EDWARD HOLLIS is an architect, a teacher and a writer, whose books include *The Secret Lives of Buildings* and *The Memory Palace: A Book of Lost Interiors*. He lives in Edinburgh, where he is Reader in Interior Design and Director of Research at Edinburgh College of Art in the University of Edinburgh.

THE SCHOOL OF LIFE is dedicated to exploring life's big questions: *How do we find fulfilling work? Can we ever understand our past? Why are relationships so hard to master? If we could change the world, should we?* Based in London, with campuses around the globe, The School of Life offers classes, therapies, books and other tools to help you create a more satisfying life. We don't have all the answers but we will direct you towards a variety of ideas from the humanities – from philosophy to literature, psychology to the visual arts – guaranteed to stimulate, provoke, nourish and console.

How to Make a Home
Edward Hollis

MACMILLAN

First published 2016 by Macmillan
an imprint of Pan Macmillan
20 New Wharf Road, London N1 9RR
Associated companies throughout the world
www.panmacmillan.com

ISBN 978-1-4472-9333-0

Pan Macmillan does not have any control
over, or any responsibility for, any author
or third party websites referred to in or on
this book.

987654321

A CIP catalogue record for this book is
available from the British Library.

Typeset by seagulls.net

Printed and bound by CPI Group (UK) Ltd,
Croydon, CR0 4YY

Visit www.panmacmillan.com to
read more about all our books and to
buy them. You will also find features,
author interviews and news of any
author events, and you can sign up for
e-newsletters so that you're always first
to hear about our new releases.

London Borough of Enfield	
91200000548832	
Askews & Holts	Jan-2016
640	£7.99

To Squid the cat, who can make herself at home anywhere

Contents

Introduction

How do you make the perfect home?

Once upon a time there lived a rich man who had everything. He possessed a happy family, a wide circle of friends, a profitable business, and a substantial reputation.

Or that's how the Viennese architect Adolf Loos used to start his story, around a hundred years ago.

At least, he'd continue, the rich man had nearly everything; he had everything except a perfect home; and so he decided to seek advice on how he should get one. He summoned a famous architect and asked him what he should do. The architect went to the rich man's house and looked around, and told him to throw out all his furniture and his clutter. He brought in an army of craftsmen and tradesmen and artists, and soon enough our rich man had the most beautiful house in the city.

Wherever he looked in his new home, he found the art of the architect: in the designer doorknobs, in the beautiful chairs, the artfully scattered cushions, the subtly patterned carpets, and in even the simple and elegant plates on which his dinner was served. The architect had thought of everything. Our rich man had a perfect home. His life, finally, was complete.

There are all sorts of books that will advise you, as Adolf Loos's architect once advised his rich man, about how to make a home. Step into the interiors section of most bookshops, and you'll find glossy guides to style, from Moroccan to Mid-Century Modern. You can find guides to the homes of the rich and famous, and catalogues of styles in French or English furniture from the eighteenth century. There will be DIY manuals for making curtains, distressing sideboards, fitting bedrooms into cupboards, rag-rolling walls, plumbing toilets and laying tables.

Literature of this kind has an ancient history. In ancient Rome, the architect Vitruvius wrote a treatise for the Emperor Augustus and the statesman Pliny described his ideal holiday house as a self-serving illustration of his domestic and moral probity. It's a literature that has echoes in the moral and domestic economies of Confucianism, the Hindu *Shilpa Shastras*, and in ideal homes from William Morris's Red House of the 1860s to Le Corbusier's machines for living in of the 1920s.

Then there are guides for the perplexed housewife, written by Mrs Beeton in the nineteenth century and Martha Stewart in the twenty-first. They provide recipes not just for food, but for household management and etiquette, dispensing advice on how to deal with servants, get stains out of carpets, or pay a social call. This advice has in common with Pliny or Confucius a conviction that domestic and moral order are aligned. After all, in traditional parlance, untidiness and immorality meet in the Slut and the Slattern.

Then there are arbiters of taste. Elsie de Wolfe, writing on decoration in early twentieth-century America, saw herself as a missionary, bringing good taste to the masses in a way that Terence Conran,

Ingvar Kamprad, Laura Ashley or Kelly Hoppen have followed since. Their harmoniously accessorized, standardized approaches to home décor seem to provide a formula or a kit, the purchase of which will help the rest of us to avoid errors in aesthetic judgement and domestic arrangement.

And finally, this sort of advice has made its way onto the television: *Changing Rooms*, asking *How Clean is your House?*, telling you not just *How to Cook* but *How to Eat*, or, to match, *What Not to Wear*, and how, in general, to *Get Your House in Order*. The drama of the TV makeover, with its limited timescale and budget, its miracles wrought with MDF, and the tearful (for better or for worse) Grand Reveal, is designed to show how the making of a home can make (or break) the people who live in it, too.

This book is not advice of that kind. Reading it will not make your home more tasteful. It will not reveal this year's colours, or next year's *chaise*. I have no clever table-laying tips or recipes to share. This is not a book about design, or not solely. There are, it will argue, no definitive laws we can use to create beauty or domestic harmony. I am not, I hope, like the architect who advised the rich man how to perfect his home.

But this book will attempt to answer the question contained in its title: how can you make a home? It's a deliberately ambiguous question, for, as we shall see, making a home, being at home, feeling at home, or making yourself at home are things we can do anywhere, any time. Home, it will argue, is less attached to bricks and mortar, cushions and curtains, than to a sense that we deserve to belong in our surroundings, to shape them, to change them, and in doing so, to dwell in them.

This book will pose six questions: How do you build a home? How do you furnish a home? How do you decorate a home? How do you collect a home? How do you keep a home? And, finally, how can you make yourself at home without having one?

These questions take us through the elements that comprise the home: firstly the architecture of the house; secondly the furniture we carry with us from house to house; thirdly, the decoration of our homes; fourthly, the clutter we collect when we make a home; fifthly, that much-unloved aspect of making a home: housework; and finally, the public sphere from which, or in which, we seek intervals of refuge and rest.

Each chapter will address assumptions that have often been made about the home: that there is such a thing as an ideal home (and that it is a house); that, at home, there should be a place for everything, and that everything should be in its place; that ornaments are crime; that there's no accounting for taste; that a woman's place is in the home; and finally, that it's good to be home alone.

But in this book, we will challenge those venerable clichés. We shall remember that most people cannot afford to build their own home; that home is in a state of perpetual motion; that taste is a political weapon; and that clutter can be cosmic. We'll look at home as drudgery, and find out that, for many, privacy is an unattainable luxury.

Along the way, we'll encounter psychoanalysts and architects, designers and film-makers, alchemists and anthropologists, philosophers, sociologists, cooks, activists and politicians, for home is a subject so fundamental that it is the province of no single sphere of enquiry. In each case, we'll critically read the advice they have dispensed to the home-makers of their time, considering what we agree with, what we must challenge, and how we can resolve the resulting dilemmas to make homes of our own.

For too long home has been idealized as a refuge from the world: ordered, where the world outside is chaotic; personal, where the world is generic; private, where the world is public. In this book, we'll explore how we can make ourselves at home in public; and how home isn't a place to which we retreat to escape the social world, but the vantage point from which we look into it. Home is not just our destination at the end of the day, but also the origin from which we go out in the morning.

For too long the ideal home has been imagined as something perfectible: an ideal object that can fit its occupants like a glove fits a hand, or a nest the blackbird that built it. In this book we'll be investigating the ways in which home is often not a fixed, or fixable, place, but is instead a situation that is made and unmade in time.

Perhaps, this book will argue, we should worry a little bit less about how to make a home, and a little bit more about how to make ourselves *at* home, for, as we'll discover, buildings, furniture, objects, and décor are less reliable than at first they seem.

It's something our rich man discovered soon enough, as he moved into his perfect home; but if you want to find out what happened, and why, and why it's worth knowing, you'll have to take my first piece of advice, and read on.

1. How to Build a Home

How to make the perfect home: drawing out an archetype.

A picture, and a word

We all know what home is, don't we?

Ask a child to imagine a home, and they will always draw the same one. There will be a path leading from the garden gate to a front door flanked by square windows, the facade surmounted by a triangular pitched roof. Look on top, and there will probably be a chimney, complete with billowing smoke.

It's a ubiquitous image that we all encounter as children, in story after story. It's the cottage from which Little Red Riding Hood sets out to meet the wolf, or Jack to sell his cow for a handful of beans. It's the house into which Goldilocks creeps to eat her porridge, or, made of gingerbread, that tempts Hansel and Gretel into the clutches of the witch. Go inside, the smoking chimney seems to tell us, and you'll find old Mother Goose telling her stories by the fireside.

It's a ubiquitous image for grownups too, repeated in the windows of estate agents, or along the streets of suburbs from the forest villages of Germany to the golf-course developments of Shenzen. It's an image that haunts architects, developers and builders who return to it again and again as the default form of home.

It's a simple building, detached from the world by a garden, guarded by four stout walls, sheltered under a roof, and warmed by a fire. It's a place of stability and order, guaranteed by the symmetrical placement of doors and windows. It's the sort of building we call a house.

In Mandarin, the character for it, pronounced 'shè' is even drawn like one: 舍. In Italian, Portuguese or Spanish we might call such an image *casa*; *maison* in French, or *Haus* in German. It's deceptively simple, both the drawing, and the word we use to name it. No wonder children can draw it so well. No wonder it gets everywhere.

But start using the word 'home' and things become more complicated. Homing pigeons fly back to the place from which they came. Sports teams play at home or away, in Britain there's a Home Secretary, and in the United States there's a department of Home-land Security. When the French want to say they're at home they say *chez nous*; the German *Heim*, like 'home' itself, means something quite distinct from *Haus*. In Hindi, the word for house, *grha*, also means 'family', and, with an accented 'a', a domestic servant. The modern Greek word for house, *spiti*, is derived from the same root as the word 'hospitality'. In Hungarian, they call home *otthon*: our place of origin. Home, these words seem to say, is where we come from, and where belong.

Pull apart the child's drawing, and you'll find a similarly knotty etymology. The house is the building from which we begin, and it's been around for so long, and has evolved over so many centuries, that it's hard to imagine where it might itself have begun.

The symmetrical facade is an invention of the Italian Renaissance of the fifteenth and sixteenth centuries – not coincidentally the age in which our modern conception of the theatre was born. It is, as the word implies, a mask, a theatre set, that disguises the messy reality of home behind an illusion of formal grandeur (go round the back of most houses, and you'll find the symmetry has fallen away). It suggests that the well-run house has a role to play in the maintenance of public order as well as private domestic harmony.

That the house should have two floors is a notion not much older than the facade that masks them. Once upon a time, in Europe anyway, most people lived in single-storey buildings that contained only one room. It was only in the later Middle Ages that other ones began to appear. As late as the eighteenth century, few of these rooms were given specific functions; and it was not until the nineteenth century that the bedrooms retreated from the public spaces of the main floor to an upper level all of their own. If the symmetrical facade of the house tells a story about the public face of home, the multiplication of rooms inside tells the opposite tale, of home as a place of private refuge.

The chimney was one result of this development. When the house consisted only of one room, people would make do with a hole in the roof and a fire directly below on the floor; but once the house acquired more and smaller rooms on several levels, such a casual approach became impracticable. The fireplace and the chimney were newfangled machines, designed to divert the sooty smoke out of specific rooms, and up to the top of the roof.

And that leaves the roof itself. It is much older than anything else. In Britain, the longhouses of the Anglo Saxons were almost all roof, and so were the homesteads of the Celts and the Iron Age people that preceded them. The African Kraal is all roof, as are the thatched houses of the marsh people of southern Iraq. Their similarity is the result of a pragmatic strategy rather than cosmic coincidence. It's much easier to make a triangular structure stand up than a rectangular one.

Take the words we use for home, take our child's drawing, and take them to pieces. Strip away the symmetrical facade, knock the rooms together, lop off the top floor, take out the chimneys, and what do we have? An almost conical thatched hut, with a fire smoking in the middle of the floor. It might look nothing like your home, or mine, but it's where they both began.

Hearth and home: origins

Even at the height of their empire, the Romans kept such a hut alongside the temples and palaces of the Forum to remind themselves of where they had come from. The thatch kept on burning down, of course, ignited by sparks from the open fire that burned in the middle of the floor, but they rebuilt it every time, just the same. They called it the *Tugurium Romuli*: the house of Romulus, the legendary founder of their city, and their first king.

And more than two thousand years ago, in his treatise on architecture, Vitruvius used the *Tugurium Romuli* to speculate on the origins of architecture itself. He lived in a world in which histories of ancient times were remembered in myths and legends rather than archives and records and so his was an imaginative reconstruction, told, like all those fairy-tale accounts of cottages in the German forest, as a story.

Once upon a time, he wrote, people lived like wild animals, wandering the wilderness. Then one day a lightning strike started a fire in the forest, and people started to gather together around it, in a circle, to warm their hands. Standing together, for the first time, in a single place, they started to talk to one another, and to share ideas about how they might settle down:

> Some made them of green boughs, others dug caves on mountainsides, and some, in imitation of the nests of swallows and the way they built, made places of refuge out of mud and twigs. Next, by observing the shelters of others and adding new details to their own inceptions, they constructed better and better kinds of huts as time went on.[1]

The *Tugurium Romuli*, observed Vitruvius, was the last relic of those immemorial days; but it was also something else, for to speculate on origins, especially mythical ones, is also to speculate on essences. The essence of the home, Vitruvius' story implied, lay not in the marbled halls and magnificent facades of his time, but in something simpler: a group of people warming themselves in the wilderness, standing and sitting around a fire, and talking to one another.

The Italians still have a special word for home: *focolare*. Search for the origins of this word, and you'll find the Latin name for hearth, which is *focus*. 'Hearth and home' we say; and when we teach children how to draw a home, they cap it off with a chimney. More than a millennium after the last copy of the first house, the *Tugurium Romuli*, disappeared in an undocumented fire, it lives on, in a word, and a childish doodle.

Go west: homes for pioneers

Home is our focus, our point of origin; and wherever we are, and whoever we are, its own point of origin remains with us still. The American architect Frank Lloyd Wright is credited with being one of the inventors of the modern house. He couldn't, on the face of it, have been more different from the savages of Vitruvius' ancient myth and their primitive huts.

Wright imagined his clients as pioneers, staking their claim to the leafy Chicago suburb of Oak Park with bricks and mortar, just as their predecessors had done to the prairie with their covered wagons; and he pioneered new houses for new people, people whose parents had run away from the old world to the new to make new lives for themselves, unencumbered by the weight of the past.

'Prairie houses', they were called, in reference to the wide empty spaces of the New World that stretched out in front of them; and with their daring cantilevers, their open-plan living spaces and their wide windows, they were places for pioneers who had left old-fashioned conventions behind them.

When Wright decided to build himself a home, he too struck out West: 'a voluntary exile, into the uncharted and unknown',[2] and being a Midwesterner himself, he found himself, ironically, going home, to the hill in the valley in Wisconsin from which he had origin- ally come. '[It] was one of my favourite places when I was a boy,' he wrote, 'for pasque flowers grew there in March sun while snow still streaked the hillsides.'[3]

Wright returned to his own place of origin; but for him it was a double returning. He called his house Taliesin, a Welsh name, in honour of the country from which his grandparents had sailed from the Old World to the New. Like an imagined America itself, the hill in the valley at Taliesin was wild and uninhabited; and Wright had no intention of disrupting its native beauty. He designed himself a house that 'would belong to that hill, as trees and ledges of rock did; as grandfather and mother had belonged to it'.[4] Taliesin was 'a house of the north. The whole was low, wide and snug, a broad shelter seeking fellowship with its surroundings.'[5] Sheltered under enormous roofs, anchored by heavy stone chimneys, literally rooted to the spot, Taliesin was everything that our child's drawing strives to be. It was home.

A myth: the poetics of houses

For children and for grownups, for ancient Romans and modern Americans, images of house and home remind us of where we've come from, and of who, therefore, we think we are. What's more, as we'll see, home makes us who we are. If we want to understand one, we must also try to understand the other.

In *The Poetics of Space*, published in 1958, the French philosopher Gaston Bachelard made the point: 'A house constitutes a body of images that give mankind proofs or illusions of stability',[6] and that, perhaps, is why that child's drawing is so compelling: it represents somewhere and something that is, unlike the world beyond the garden gate, unchanging.

The Poetics of Space is ostensibly a rummage through a typical house, with a cellar, two floors for living in, and an attic; but it is also a meditation on how we use such a house to make ourselves a home in the wider world. 'Our house,' wrote Bachelard, 'is our first universe, a real cosmos in every sense of the word.'[7]

And that cosmos is no abstract philosophical idea. 'The house we were born in is physically inscribed in us,' wrote Bachelard, as 'a group of organic habits. After twenty years, in spite of all the other anonymous stairways, we would recapture the reflexes of the "first stairway", we would not stumble on that rather high step . . . the feel of the tiniest latch has remained in our hands.'[8]

We imagine that buildings are passive objects made by human hands; but, Bachelard argues, in fact the very reverse happens. The way our hands (and by extension the rest of our bodies) feel their way around the spaces we live in is formed by the first space they ever touched, the building from which we begin: home. Like the Hungarian *Otthon*, or the Italian *Focolare*, home is our point of origin: the navel of the world we each grow to inhabit.

'A great many of our memories are housed,' wrote Bachelard, 'and if the house is a bit elaborate, if it has a cellar and a garret, nooks and crannies, our memories have refuges that are all the more clearly delineated.'[9] Try to imagine the house he is describing: it's a slightly more elaborate, picturesque version of the child's drawing we started with. One is tempted to think of some turreted nineteenth-century house in the provincial suburbs of northern France: the very sort of house in which Bachelard himself grew up.

But the form of this imaginary house was not just the result of autobiographical musing. Bachelard was something of an apostle of psychoanalysis, and his home was constructed as metaphor for the id, ego and superego and all the rest of it. 'The conscious acts like a man,' he quoted Jung as saying, 'who hearing a suspicious noise in the cellar, hurries to the attic, and, finding no burglars there, decides, consequently, that the noise was pure imagination. In reality, this prudent man did not dare venture into the cellar.'[10]

And that lends a very particular structure to Bachelard's imaginary house. In the middle is a 'conscious' region of the house – the ego – in which daily life is lived. It is framed by two other spaces: an attic above, cluttered with the desiccated *memoriae* of the superego; and a cellar below, whose damp and dark excite the unnameable terrors and insatiable desires of the id.

Home represents stability in an unstable world. Home is a metaphor for the self. Home is the storehouse of memory. Home is made by, and makes us, what we are. Home is where we can be ourselves. There's nothing naive about that child's drawing, with its brick box at the end of the garden path, with its triangular roof and its smoking chimney; and it's not just a drawing of a building. It's a drawing of who you think you are.

A reality: superimposed boxes

But like the farmyard noises with which urban children who've never seen a cow or heard a duck learn to speak, the archetype of the house they learn to draw (and which we dream of building as adults) is a rarity. Very few of us can afford to build ourselves a home that stands in a garden, as a building on its own, with two floors, and a roof, and a chimney.

How to make a home in the modern city: apartment living in contemporary Shanghai.

'In Paris,' wrote Bachelard, 'there are no houses, and the inhabitants of the big city live in superimposed boxes.' He didn't approve: 'The number of the street and the floor give the location of our conventional hole, but our abode has neither space around it nor verticality inside it.'[11] That is to say, the mass-produced housing in which most of us live lacks the psychological breadth and depth of a detached house.

Your dream home might still be a house, detached from the world, sitting in a garden with a roof and a chimney; but it's becoming increasingly unlikely that you or I will live in one. In 2014, the World Health Organization noted that 54 per cent of humanity now live in cities. That is a figure that has grown by 20 per cent since 1960,[12] and it is projected to keep on growing. Inside those cities individual houses are themselves increasingly rare. For example, London might once have been a city of terraced houses, but as property prices rise in relation to income those houses have been subdivided into flats, and new dwellings are built in shared blocks rather than as individual units. In much of the world, from the *insulae* of imperial Rome to the *khiva* villages of the Pueblo Indians of New Mexico, urbanites have been living in flats since ancient times.

Bachelard's link between house, home and self might work for the forest-dwelling, hut-building savages of Vitruvius' myth, or the tiny elite who can afford to commission a Frank Lloyd Wright to design and build them a Taliesin, but it's not going to work for the rest of us. If you live in a flat, it's unlikely that it was built with precisely you or me in mind. Most of us make ourselves at home in places which were never really designed for us in the first place.

But, somehow, making do, keeping what we must, changing what we can, we manage. We change what we find, and in doing so, make it our own.

Altered states: time and the architecture of home

Around the same time that Wright was dreaming up Taliesin, Adolf Loos, the author of our story about the rich man, decided to advertise a tour of the homes that he had designed in Vienna. He was working in the crowded, twilit capital of an ancient empire rather than on an empty prairie; and the homes he'd made were quite different to those that Wright had designed. They weren't even much like the home he'd conjured up in his story.

At Herr T's apartment on the second floor of 19 Wohlleben-gasse, on the corner with Alleegasse, was a smoking room lined with mahogany panelling, and an integrated sideboard 'with many corners'[13] to mask the crookedness of an existing party wall. He'd created Herr L's dining room on the third floor of 13 Opernring by knocking two rooms together.

'The cross beam was clad with mahogany,' Loos reported, 'and, for the sake of symmetry, this cladding was repeated, thus creating a ceiling with wooden beams.'[14] Herr S's smoking room on the fifth floor of Elizabethstrasse was created by knocking together two rooms, too, and the junction between them was disguised with a fireplace. In Herr K's apartments on the second floor of 13 Nibelun-gengasse, the old bathroom was converted into a new vestibule, and painted yellow and white.

Wright was a romantic who dreamed of every home as an individual work of art. The homes in Loos's description, on the other hand, were all contingent affairs, cobbled together from party walls set at funny angles that had to be disguised with cleverly designed sideboards or fireplaces, or structural beams that must be clad in timber, or bathrooms that must be converted into vestibules.

Loos might have been an architect, but the homes he'd created weren't really the product of architecture at all. They were acts of improvisation, alteration, and negotiation with what already exists. Loos's genius lay not in inventing new buildings, but in taking existing, generic ones – the superimposed boxes of Bachelard's disapproving description of Paris – and turning them, somehow, into individualized spaces created for individual people: into homes.

Deep time, deep home

If you're reading this in the inner suburbs of London, or Paris, or New York, or Melbourne, Mumbai or Buenos Aires, then Loos's apartments will sound familiar to you. It is likely that, like the tenements of the Vienna Ringstrasse, your home is older than you are, and that the people who designed it – and the people for whom it was designed, along with all their foibles and customs – are long gone. Not only was your home not designed for you, it probably wasn't even designed for the society you live in.

Let's return to the terraced or semi-detached houses of suburban London. They are ordinary enough and the majority of Londoners live in buildings like them, as do their counterparts in the inner suburbs of many other cities. Think of them as they are now, opened out to the garden at the back with a deck or a terrace, the front room knocked through to the room behind it to create a family room, heated, lit, connected to Wi-Fi, television and the sewage network.

And think of them a hundred years ago, when the garden was a drying green and the place for the outside lavatory (there wasn't an inside one), the front room was a gloomy overstuffed museum of bric-a-brac kept for best, damp streamed down the windows and walls in the morning, and light flickered from smoky gas lamps. Visit the very house you live in today when it had just been built, and it would most probably seem utterly alien, if not uninhabitable.

And that's just an ordinary house only a century old. Imagine living in an apartment building in Rome. The flats at the Via del Teatro Marcello were built as a public theatre in the time of Augustus, and those on the Salita del Grillo have been converted from a medieval castle, which was itself built on top of the ruins of ancient shopping centres. The apartment buildings of the Piazza Navona started out two thousand years ago as the seats of an ancient race track.

Give it enough time, and time makes a curious nonsense of building a home, since it proves that we can build our homes anywhere, and anyhow. Houses last longer than the life of any single person or any single style of life, and as a consequence, the correspondence between the form and the function of any home can only ever be temporary. The homes we make in them are ephemeral affairs that remind us that building a home often involves rebuilding somebody else's.

So where does that leave Bachelard's neat idea that the house and the self correspond with one another? What has happened to our child's drawing?

The passage of time was something of which the psychoanalysts, like Carl Jung, who inspired Bachelard, were well aware; and when Jung argued that the self was like a house, he was keen to show that there was nothing eternal, or stable, about either of them. He described instead a model for both that was nothing like our neat little box of a house. The upper storey of *his* house of the self, he explained, was Victorian, built on an older, sixteenth-century foundation:

> A careful examination of the masonry discloses the fact that it was reconstructed from a dwelling tower of the eleventh century. In the cellar we discover a Roman foundation wall, and under the cellar a filled-in cave, in the floor of which stone tools are found and remnants of glacial fauna in the layers below.[15]

Blackbirds and cuckoos

Both our concept of self and of the house possess many layers of reinvention and re-creation. They are entirely specific to our own presents, and rooted in pasts that are much older than we are. They survive by being passed from generation to generation, preserved and altered with every passing.

So making yourself at home isn't as simple as building a building called a house. We often call homemaking 'nesting'; but that old idea has to take a new turn. When you make yourself a home, you are not the blackbird building a nest of your own, customized to your every whim and foible. You are the cuckoo, who makes a speciality of occupying the nest that someone else has made, and altering it to suit your own needs. It's something we all do, and, in turn, someone else will to do it to us, too.

When we make ourselves at home, we take an existing building – individual or mass-produced, new or old, permanent or temporary – and by hook or by crook, we find a way of living in it. As we shall discover, we do this by installing furniture, hoarding objects, painting the walls, or scrubbing the floor. All of these enterprises are acts of making home; but they aren't acts of building a building: they are acts of altering one.

Whatever children draw – a house, a building, architecture – cannot, on its own, make a home. They are just the beginning.

2. How to Furnish a Home

How to make a home under the table.

A bedroom camp

When I was a child I used to play a game. I'd take all my bedroom furniture and move it around. Then I'd drape it with blankets and bed sheets, so that within my room, I'd constructed another one, rather like a Bedouin tent. Then I'd crawl in, and lie there on the floor, and eat a midnight feast in the camp I'd created for myself.

It drove my parents mad: not least because there I was crunching crisps long after my bedtime; not least, I might add, because the camp was child-sized and they couldn't get into it to extract me. Instead, they'd stand at the door and shout at me to return everything to its proper place and get into mine – my bed.

It always felt unfair. I wasn't really doing anything they'd never done. After all, when we'd moved in a matter of months before, they had done much the same thing, unloading furniture, and moving it into empty rooms, and moving it around, and moving it around again until they said they were happy to settle in.

Just like them, I had taken a generic architectural box and turned it into a world of my own that fitted me more precisely. Within a house, just as they had, I had made a home. They didn't see it that way, of course. 'There's a place for everything,' they said, and they made me put everything back in its place.

I suspect most of us have an inner parent that agrees with them, and an inner child that would rather make a camp. After all, the architecture of a house is only just the beginning of a home. Dining rooms only become dining rooms once a table and chairs are set out in the middle of them and sitting rooms only when the sofa arrives. Bedrooms are, in English anyway, named for a piece of furniture. Buildings without furniture are empty vessels. They only become homes once we furnish them to suit our specific needs.

Deck the hall

There's nothing naughty about it, really: I was only doing something that everyone has been doing for years. Up until the eighteenth century in Edinburgh, for example, rooms in ordinary houses weren't even given names. They were either called 'rooms', 'fire rooms' (that is to say they had a fireplace in them), 'garrets', 'closets' or 'cellars'. Only once these rooms were furnished did they acquire a function, and then only temporarily, until the furniture within them was rearranged and the function changed once again.

Once upon a time, remember, houses consisted of nothing more than one room: a hall with a fire in the middle of the floor. It fell to furniture temporarily arranged within it to articulate what was actually going to happen there. Just as I did with my childhood camp, large households would camp out in the great hall, arranging benches and tables and tapestries to cordon off areas for private functions and public meetings.

Little tents of tapestry, for example, would be contrived under the hammer-beam roofs to create islands of quiet amid the melee: around beds, or places for women. Important people would sit on thrones separated from the rest of the room by the use of parquets, literally 'little parks' of precious material arranged on the floor, or by canopies suspended overhead. The servants whose job it was to rig them up were known as upholsterers.

These usages survive today in the figures of speech we associate with the practice of the law and business. British legal advocates are called to the bar, which was once, literally, a wooden bar set up to divide the ordinary functions of the hall from judicial meetings. Judges sit on the 'bench', although that particular piece of furniture has long since been replaced by a more comfortable chair. Indeed, chairs themselves were so unusual in the Middle Ages that the only person who was allowed to sit in one in any hall was the chairman of the board, which was, in those days, an actual board, mounted on trestles, around which business meetings were held.

The architecture of the hall might have been shedlike, but once it was furnished, it made a model of social order that stretched all the way from the beggar standing at the door to the chairman of the board sitting in his throne at the high table at the other end of the room. Above the king's throne in the Great Hall in Winchester Castle was painted the same wheel of fortune to which both beggar and lord, both high and low, were bound, as if to remind both of them that their positions might switch with one capricious turn.

The hierarchical patterns these arrangements of furniture made were much more permanent than the furniture itself, little of which survives. Go to important state occasions at Westminster Hall in

London today, and you'll find the Queen sitting in precisely the same place (if not in exactly the same chair) her ancestors have sat in for centuries. There's only one time the monarch was ever asked to sit anywhere else, and that was during the trial of Charles I, in which representatives of the people sat in the place of the throne, and the king sat in their usual place, as the accused. They executed him.

'There should be a place for everything, and everything should be in its place,' we say, and the saying applies as equally to modern homes as to medieval great halls. If an unfurnished room is an empty box, and a furnished one the precise reflection of its particular function, then it stands to reason: if you want to know how to furnish a home properly, you'll need to know where everything, and everyone, is going to go.

In the last chapter, we started with the idea of the individual house as an archetype of selfhood, stability and order. We discovered, however, that like many archetypes such a house is a myth: few of us build ourselves individual homes. Instead we make do, making ourselves at home in all sorts of buildings that were built long before we ever encountered them.

The means we use to occupy them are rarely architectural. Instead, like the upholsterers of the Middle Ages or myself as a child, we rearrange the furniture and build a camp.

A machine for living in

No writer on the home could have been less medieval than that irascible prophet of modern architecture Le Corbusier; but he was quite as much a stickler for domestic order as his ancestors. It was he who coined the idea that the house is 'a machine for living in',[1] and in his treatise of 1923, 'Towards a New Architecture', he compared the home to that most modern of machines of his time, the aeroplane.

It wasn't an aesthetic comparison: Le Corbusier didn't want houses to look like planes or machines. The lesson of the aeroplane, he argued, didn't lie in what it looked like, but rather in the way in which its design solved a particular problem no one had ever thought of before. People had been able to fly since the Montgolfier brothers launched their hot-air balloon in 1783, but they hadn't been able to control where they were going to go.

The aeroplane, with its directional body and wings, changed all that. 'When a problem is properly stated, in our epoch, it inevitably finds its solution',[2] wrote Le Corbusier. The inventors of the aeroplane, he observed, had created their wonderful new machine by asking themselves what it was for, rather than what it should look like.

The problem of the house, he continued, was that the reverse had happened: everyone knew what home should look like; but no one had really thought about what it was for. Look at Victorian houses, with their turrets and their clutter, think of our child's drawing, and it's all too easy to see what he was talking about.

'Let us shut our eyes to what exists,'[3] he commanded; and he described what he thought home was for: 'a receptacle for light and sun . . . a surface over which one can walk at ease, a bed on which to stretch yourself, a chair in which to rest or work, a work table, receptacles in which each thing can be put at once in its right place.'[4] It's a disarmingly simple vision.

Just like an aeroplane, which needs to be as light as possible to stay in the air, the components of Le Corbusier's modern home were minimized: 'Demand bare walls in your bedroom, your living room and your dining room,' he commanded, 'built-in fittings to take the place of much of the furniture, which is expensive to buy, takes up too much room, and needs looking after . . . Buy only practical furniture and never buy decorative "pieces". If you want to see bad taste, go into the houses of the rich.'[5]

And just as with the moving parts of any efficient machine, Le Corbusier also believed that, in this house, there should be a place for everything, and that everything should be kept in its place. 'Never undress in your bedroom,' he commanded. 'It is not a clean thing to do and makes the room horribly untidy . . . demand fitments for your linen and clothing, not more than 5 feet in height, with drawers, hangers etc. . . . . Keep your odds and ends in drawers or cabinets.'[6]

The furniture of the modern home was conceived as the working parts of a machine; and Le Corbusier's own designs for furniture certainly fit the bill. Constructed of black leather and tubular chrome-plated steel, they have all the charming whimsy of surgical equipment. The modern home, it seems, had all the military discipline and mechanical efficiency that Le Corbusier so admired in the aeroplanes of World War I.

Even that mythologist of Hearth and Home, Frank Lloyd Wright, agreed and in a rare, reflective, rueful moment, he admitted that his skills as an architect did not stretch to the design or the arrangement of furniture:

I soon found it difficult, anyway, to make some of the furniture in the 'abstract'; that is, to design it as architecture and make it human at the same time – fit for human use. I have been black and blue in some spot, somewhere, almost all my life from too intimate contacts with my own furniture.[7]

Furniture, however efficient, ordered, machinelike, built-in, or co-ordinated, possesses, as we shall see, a life of its own. Like all machines, the 'machine for living in' is bound to go wrong.

You are the ghost in the machine

And that's where the fun starts.

Mon Oncle, Jacques Tati's 1958 film, begins so well. It all starts in a designer home, in a designer suburb, where, apparently, everything runs as smoothly as a machine, there's a place for everything, and everything is in its place.

It is morning. A housewife comes to the front door of a modern house, carrying a feather duster. Her besuited husband and her uniformed son are standing there, and before she kisses them goodbye, she dusts them down. They drive off in a designer car to the factory and the school, and she, clad in a hygienic housecoat, sets about cleansing their antiseptic dwelling with a vacuum cleaner of the most modern design. It all begins so well: with a mechanical Corbusian dream.

But then the eponymous uncle appears. He has a job in his brother-in-law's factory, but somehow, he can't get the machine he is employed to oversee to work. While it should be producing perfect plastic piping, he somehow manages to get it to spit out sausage links with knots, and twists, bulges and kinks so egregious that the machine itself eventually gives up in a cloud of steam, and the factory grinds to a halt. Uncle isn't good with machines, you see.

He's not much good with order altogether. At the end of the day, he picks his nephew up from school; and instead of taking him straight back to his hygienic home, he takes him off to play with some filthy street kids on a piece of waste ground. It is only several hours later that they appear back at the house, the little boy smeared in chocolate, knees covered in mud. His mother stands him on a mat and vacuums him down before she lets him back into the house.

And that's when the fun starts. You see, Uncle can't resist poking around his sister's modern machine of a home: jumping back, startled, as cabinets fly open in response to motion sensors, playing curiously with the unbreakable plastic utensils until, of course, he drops one on the floor, and it proves to be the one breakable object in the whole kitchen. Exiled outside, he prunes the geometric topiary in the garden until there's nothing left of it, and, breaking the fountain, brings chaos to an elegant tea party his sister has so carefully arranged.

It's all too much for all of them. At the end of the day, our uncle tips an uncomfortable modernist sofa on its side, and falls asleep on it, his snores echoing round the clinical house as if it were the most comfortable *chaise longue* in the world. The next morning, he is sent back to where he came from, so that he can do no more damage to their ordered, efficient lives.

And that's where the fun finally starts. You see, Uncle doesn't live in a machine. Instead, he follows the stray dogs through a crack in the wall that surrounds the neat suburbs, and finds himself in the middle of town. The streets are filthy: the street sweeper is too busy chatting with passersby to keep them clean. The town square is crowded with a pleasingly aimless crowd of maiden aunts, irascible postmen, unruly schoolboys, and flirtatious ingénues, all not going about their business, whatever business that might be, if any at all.

And so the uncle enters a decrepit apartment building, and ascends to his garret up a staircase of bewildering, tortuous, and, of course, inefficient complexity. Just as he reaches the top of the staircase, he leans over to open a window by his front door that stands slightly ajar. A patch of light moves on the crumbling wall; there's a birdcage hanging there, and as the light moves, the bird contained within it begins to sing.

It's a tiny adjustment – designed by no one, imagined by no one, the result of a coincidental accident. It's a mechanical movement, to be sure, but not part of the machinery of a home ever imagined by a Corbusier or a Wright.

Homes aren't just machines, and what they contain – the lives we lead in them – can't be manufactured as if they were. In fact, as suggested by Mon Oncle's little window or the sofa which is much more comfortable once it is upended on its side, things often work best when they are not being used for the purposes for which they were designed.

Sometimes furniture is at its most effective when there isn't a place for everything, and everything isn't in its place. After all, furniture is the thing that allows us to make the rooms of our houses do all sorts of things they were never originally intended to. Furniture isn't just there to fulfil functions, or to solve problems:

it can restate them too, just as the aeroplane once restated the problem of flight.

Meubles and immeubles

It's something our medieval ancestors knew, setting up camp as they did in their draughty halls, centuries ago; and their attitude survives in the modern word for furniture in many European languages: *meubles* in French and *mobili* in Italian, for example. 'Moveable', the words mean, in distinction to the fixed, *immeuble* buildings that will house them.

Furniture is mobile in two dimensions. Firstly, and most obviously, we can move furniture around within the home.

Furniture allows us to repurpose spaces without knocking down a single wall; and it allows us to do it in minutes. In the eighteenth century, for example, light and elegant chairs would be arranged around the walls of rooms and were only taken out when needed. As a result, rooms could take on diverse functions in a single day. There was no necessity to describe them as anything other than 'rooms'.

Things only started to change in the nineteenth century: there's an account of a house whose owners had subscribed to the novel fad of leaving the furniture out in the middle of the room, permanently. One guest was so outraged he complained about the lazy servants who hadn't moved it to its proper place against the walls. By the time of Le Corbusier's manual, furniture was something that should be built-in.

It reminds me, a little, of the camps I used to build when I was a child – and of my parents' impatience with them. Like Mon Oncle,

I was removing things from their proper places, arranging them as they weren't intended to be arranged, and using them for things they weren't meant to be used for. Furniture, of its nature, invites disobedience, misuse, and play.

My parents shouldn't have been displeased. They were doing exactly the same thing: with the chair in the bedroom that had become an impromptu hanger for the laundry they'd only worn once and didn't want to put in the wash; when they stood on the kitchen table to change the light bulb; or went to sleep on the sofa on a Sunday afternoon.

They shouldn't have been angry. After all, it was easy enough to move everything back again, and, what is more, that is exactly what they were doing downstairs: moving the sofas back against the walls when there was a party, grabbing a mismatched chair to make up numbers around the table at dinner, or carrying the deckchairs and an old card table outside into the garden when it was sunny.

Home on the move

But furniture doesn't just get moved around within the home, it is moved from home to home too.

Medieval households lived on the road, moving every few months to another castle or hall in search of food, or military advantage. Everyone would come: they'd take their family, and their servants, and their clothes; but they'd also take all their furniture. Sometimes they even took the windows: the glass in them was so precious that, often, they could only afford one set. They'd arrive at some fortress or other, their upholsterers would get to work with poles and tapestries, benches and tables, and soon enough, a bare stone shell would be transformed into a habitable home. When the lord left, it would disappear along with him.

In fact any furniture that remained behind – sometimes the throne, for example, or the table of judgement that stood before it – was so unusual that it would be made of marble, and given a special name – *dormant* – to refer to the fact that it *didn't* move.

More of us are cuckoos than blackbirds. Just as very few of us actually design and build our nests, but instead, occupy ones made by and for others, so very few of us could claim to live in homes for which our furniture was designed. Instead, we make use of the furniture we already have, and which we have brought with us from the other homes we have occupied before.

Adolf Loos admired the practice: 'An English bride would most of all like to take her parents' furniture with her. Here in Vienna brides are deaf to the suggestion that they would make things financially easier for their parents if they took over something of their furniture. They want to have something "new", "fashionable", "modern". They even want something "artist designed".'[8]

Like Loos's English brides, most of us, I suspect, carry our furniture with us from house to house. My kitchen table is an old door, nicked from the art college where I work. The chairs around it were ordered online, and arrived in the mail. The old armchair that sits facing them in the kitchen is something I inherited from my grandmother, and she from hers. It has probably sat in around ten sitting rooms along the way. I drove it up here in a white van two years ago.

Like an English bride's, my home is neither new, nor fashionable, nor artist designed; but it is mine. Through the medium of furniture, my kitchen – once upon a time a generic box designed in the 1950s by the City of Edinburgh council for the generic Edinburgh council-house tenant – has been transformed by a collage of things old, new and borrowed, if not blue, into something which could have been created by no one else but me.

Forty years on, I'm still camping out at home.

Home is a camp

Homes are, like the tents erected in medieval great halls or my impromptu bedroom camp, temporary affairs, hasty arrangements, attempts to customize the more permanent architecture we live in to serve our own particular purposes. As those purposes change, so do the pieces of furniture that articulate them within the rooms of our homes.

But it moves in another way too. Our ancestors, the very distant ones, wandering German forest or American prairie or Asiatic steppe, were all nomads once, and now, centuries later, as we flit from perch to perch in the cities of the contemporary world, we still are. Like them, even when we're at home, we move home around with us.

It is, I hope, a liberating proposition. As Loos put it:

It is ridiculous to lay down to people where a thing should stand, design everything for them from the lavatory pan to the ashtray. On the contrary, I like people to move their

Making home on the move: tables and chairs set out at an Airstream trailer gathering, 1961.

furniture around so that it suits them (not me!), and it is quite natural (and I approve) when they bring the old pictures and mementos they have come to love into a new interior, irrespective of whether they are good taste or bad.[9]

Furniture is the first of the devices we use to occupy the permanent buildings in which we make our temporary homes. Furniture is, and allows us to be, disobedient, contingent, playful and irreverent, subverting and individualizing the order of houses in order to make ourselves at home. This is a continuous process of readjustment, as capricious, as changeable, as we are.

Home isn't something we build: it is something we bring with us.

3. How to Decorate a Home

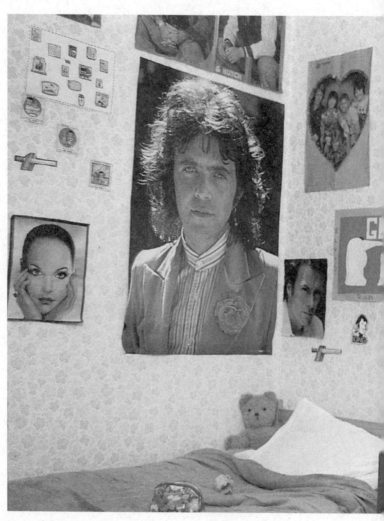

How to decorate a home: posters, pin-ups and teenage dreams, 1977.

A camp bedroom

A decade after I'd built my childhood camps I was still rearranging things in my bedroom; but this time I was a teenager, I'd saved up my pocket money, and my efforts were on a grander scale. I sanded and varnished the floor. I painted the walls a pale sky blue; and, using thin white lines, divided them into a system of panelling, and hung them with black-and-white prints. I painted all the furniture white, and insisted on white curtains and white bed linen. I hung white muslin draperies over the bed so that it resembled a four-poster; and ornamented it with silver cushions, made by blowing up the empty insides of old wine boxes.

My parents would come in and look around; but now, instead of shouting at me to put everything back in its place, they would smile a little. 'It's all, er, wonderfully *theatrical* . . .' they would say, and then their voices would trail off. 'Keep going,' they'd murmur; and then they would leave the room.

They were right. My bedroom was theatrical; looking back on it, I now realize, perhaps comically so. The whole room had the atmosphere of a tart's boudoir, albeit the very tasteful boudoir, I would have said at the time, of a high-class courtesan in the age of Louis XV.

It was a look I had carefully contrived. I'd spent days lying on my bed, flicking through glossy magazines like *Architectural Digest* and *World of Interiors*, or gazing longingly at luscious films like *Diva* and *Dangerous Liaisons*, salivating over the heavily styled salons of continental *chatelaines* and the loft apartments of bohemian millionaires. I guess that was what made my parents smile: we lived in neither a chateau nor a Park Avenue apartment, and I was a teenage boy, albeit a somewhat *theatrical* one, rather than a lady who lunched.

In fact, looking back, I was a typical teenager: one whose aspirations were as wildly out of phase with my realities as anyone else's. You might have loved the Cure and painted the walls black. You might have gone for the Disney Princess look or the sporting-trophy room. I went for rococo boudoir; but my parents, to their credit, didn't disapprove. They could see that, however theatrical it might all have been, I had attempted to make a work of art, resolving, through juxtapositions of paint colour, pattern, light and furniture, my bedroom into a harmonious whole. 'Perhaps you should be an interior decorator,' they would remark from time to time, 'you've got great taste.'

I agreed, of course: I thought I had exquisite taste, and I thought I knew what that meant. Even at that time I was aware that making a home isn't just about occupying buildings, or furnishing rooms. Home is more than a collection of places and functions; and home should be more than the sum of its parts.

A good decorator has an eye for combinations of things: of space, furniture and objects, of colour and pattern, light, and times of the day. The really good decorator is an alchemist, making from media no more precious than paint and paper, atmosphere, taste, harmony and resonance, and, ultimately, beauty. It's a mysterious magic.

That the metaphors for that magic are so mixed bears testament to just what subtle and mysterious senses the art of home décor can create. As taste it can be bitter, sweet, salt or sour; as atmosphere, it is a vapour; as harmony, it vibrates in the air and falls on the ear, as beauty, it resides in the eye of the beholder. Each of these metaphors has a long history all of its own, from taste to atmosphere, harmony to the more abstract concept of beauty itself, yet all of their riches might be generated by nothing more than the way a cushion contrasts with a chair, or matches the curtains.

Can you taste taste?

Elsie de Wolfe, born in New York in 1865, knew she was going to be a decorator from a very young age; but she didn't go to university to study interior decoration. Instead, she started her career at home on Gramercy Park, serving meals so delicious, in a setting so exquisitely decorated, that all the ladies who lunched there would ask Miss de Wolfe to make over their own houses (and their own lunches) in the same manner.

One thing led to another, and soon enough she was Lady Mendl, a member of the European aristocracy and an international sensation, the self-professed foundress of the profession of interior decorating, and the author of classic guides to home decoration including *The House in Good Taste* and, of course, *Elsie de Wolfe's Recipes for Successful Dining*.

The latter was, just as the title said, a recipe book. Each page showed a dish, or a meal – and what meals they were: boiled tongue *a la Ritz*, creamed haddock, and Indian sardine squares. But it wasn't just the food that Lady Mendl had designed. The crockery upon which it was served, the cutlery that was used to eat it, the table cloth, the table, and the chairs on which the guests would sit were all part of the recipe too, as was the backdrop of the room in which the dish was going to be eaten.

To dine – and by extension to live – in good taste, the book seemed to say, was to create a miniature, temporary, synaesthetic work of art, that addressed not just taste itself, but the other senses too: sight, touch, and even sound.

It wasn't Elsie de Wolfe's idea, however unshakeable her self-belief. Even in the most ancient cultures, taste has long been used as a metaphor for beauty. In Sanskrit, the word for flavour, *rasa*, was used to describe modes of classical dance and of emotional register in sacred sculpture. Medieval scholastics had a saying about the mysteries of taste: *De gustibus non disputandum*, they used to say – there's no accounting for it.

Can you breathe atmosphere?

So let's try another metaphor to understand what's going on. The earth's atmosphere itself is invisible but its effects on the visible are palpable: in the difference, for example, between a tropical sunset and a crystalline winter's day. The effect of climate is something that painters have long been aware of, particularly Romantics like J. M. W. Turner, who developed his expertise painting stories at sea. *The Fighting Temeraire*, for example, is towed into port for the last time under a blazing sunset; while the horrible spectacle of *Slavers Throwing Overboard the Dead and the Dying* is depicted in the midst of an infernal storm. Later on, Turner applied the expertise he learned out on the water to images of homes, too. Nothing captures the stuffy torpor, the gloomy grandeur of an afternoon in a country house like his *Interior of Petworth House*.

The atmosphere's effects on the way we feel are also tangible: think of the tension that builds before an August storm, the bad tempers of a blustery autumn morning, or the sleeplessness of clear nights under the full moon. In nature, atmospheric conditions dictate the sensory appearance of things, which in turn affects our mood.

But in the decoration of our homes, the reverse process happens. We talk of some colours, for example, as sunny or others as cold, as if they dictated weather systems all of their own; but we also use these words to describe temperaments, as if the rooms we decorate could create the dispositions of the people who inhabit them.

Can you hear harmony?

The Italian writer Mario Praz, whose *Filosofia Dell'Arredamento* was translated into English as the rather more pragmatic *Illustrated History of Interior Decoration*, struggled, in the introduction to his book, to explain what it was he was trying to write a history of. It wasn't, he was sure, merely a history of architecture or furniture. Rather it was a history of the moods that were created when they came together. He called the interiors he was writing about 'resonance chambers for the soul',¹ and he also used a very particular word for the feelings they conjured up when they resonated in this way.

Stimmung he called them. The word means, literally, 'tuning', as an orchestra might tune up to a perfect 'A' before a concert. It can also mean the single note – almost a ringing, a drone or a hum – which forms the atmospheric background to any piece of orchestral music by Romantic composers like Wagner. *Stimmung* is a participle of the verb *stimmen* – to ring – and as well as having acoustic connotations, it refers to truth: '*das stimmt*', they say in German: 'that rings true'. The mood of a room, for Praz, wasn't something seen. It was heard.

Praz wasn't the first to make the connection. The association between beauty and music dates back to ancient Greece, when Pythagoras discovered that harmonies that were pleasing to the ear were the product of simple mathematical ratios. Pluck two strings, one double the length of the other, and they would sound an octave apart. Change the ratio to 2:3 and the harmony would become a perfect fifth. Change it to 3:4 and it would sound a perfect fourth, and so on. Repeat the ratios with glasses of water or bells cast in bronze, and they would produce exactly the same harmonies. The mathematics rang true every time.

Pythagoras' discovery was a crucial step in our understanding of beauty, for the artists and architects who followed him extended his argument. If, say, 1:2 or 2:3 were beautiful proportions in music, it was argued, would they not also please the eye? The idea was taken up by architects and artists in ancient Greece, whose temples and even whose sculpted gods were subjected to rigid and minute systems of proportion. Those systems were written down by Vitruvius, and then again in the Italian Renaissance, by humanist scholars like Francesco di Giorgio, Leon Battista Alberti and Andrea Palladio. Those laws of harmony and proportion have underpinned the canons of classical art and architecture ever since.

The idea that beauty, like musical harmony, is an objective matter remains present in Mario Praz's concept of *Stimmung*, mood, atmosphere and ultimately, good taste. When we talk about harmony, proportion, balance, and all the rest of it, we are restating a belief that beauty is something objective, verifiable, and, as a consequence, repeatable. Beauty rings true.

Laws of beauty

Elsie de Wolfe might have proclaimed herself founder of the profession of interior decoration in the early twentieth century, but she knew that the practice had an older history, and she was the first to admit that her own standards of taste were derived from a more venerable source. It's the same one that inspired me as a teenager.

She'd learned it on shopping trips around the chateaux of France, picking up eighteenth-century furniture for a song from aristocrats impoverished by a century of revolution. She even ended up living there in the end, in a villa she named Trianon for the exquisite home that Marie Antoinette had made for herself before she was deposed.

Elsie de Wolfe is not alone, for if there's one time and place we associate with good taste, it's eighteenth-century France. That that taste, an elegant combination of discreet gilding, elegant shades of grey, mirror, crystal and parquet, has become something of a global standard, repeatable, verifiable, and objective, is entirely deliberate, for that is precisely what it was created to become.

It was born in the late seventeenth century as part of Louis XIV's strategy of absolute monarchy, in academies and manufactories established to standardize knowledge about all things: the sciences, literature, industry and the visual arts. These academies are still with us today; and to be elected to the Académie Française is still one of the highest honours that can be bestowed by the French state.

The scholars of Louis XIV's *académie* inherited from Pythagoras, Vitruvius, and the Italian Renaissance the idea that beauty is a fixed, objective, universal, and ultimately mathematical matter of proportion and harmony. Thus it had been in the golden days of ancient Rome, and thus it should be in modern France. Art and design, they believed, should obey fixed laws; and then they set themselves the task of defining those laws.

It was a more complex task than they imagined; for as one of their number, the architect Claude Perrault, observed in his introduction to the works of Vitruvius, modern architecture, even the most beautiful modern architecture, 'has changed some of the Dispositions and Proportions which were observed by the *Ancient* and *Antique* Architects'.[2] Even so, it was generally agreed to be beautiful, just the same.

It seems, on the face of it, a minor footnote; but it had revolutionary implications for the Académie, for Perrault's observation mounted a direct challenge to the authority of the ancients. If beauty could be achieved by disobeying the ancient laws of classical art, as well as by obeying them, were those laws perhaps not as universal as they might appear, and were there other universal laws of beauty, as yet undiscovered?

Perrault took the argument further. Perhaps it was not barbarity, poverty, or ignorance that caused the modern architects of his time to disobey the laws of Vitruvius. Perhaps, he proposed, they did it on purpose, because they thought it would be more beautiful to do it that way. Perhaps, he wondered, the laws of beauty were not eternal after all, but were instead conventions, continuously shifting in response to social, historical, and geographical circumstances.

It started with a footnote, but Perrault's distinction between what he called 'positive' or absolute beauty and 'arbitrary' or conventional beauty reframed the task of Louis XIV's *académie*, for if there were no such things as fixed, eternal laws of beauty, then its job was not to discover some universal standard, but instead to invent customs and conventions for their own times.

The taste of the *Ancien Regime*, as it changed from the heavy pomposity of the interiors of Louis XIV, to the lighter frivolity of Louis XV, to the (relative) simplicity of Louis XVI, represented an evolution in conventions of arbitrary beauty. This evolution was a deliberate creation of the French state, dictated to stimulate the economy by driving the production of luxury goods, from furniture to fashion.

The decoration of houses was dictated by conventions and, in some cases, laws about what could or could not be sat on, or lived in, by whom. Gold and white, for example, were the preserve of the crown in both dress and interior décor. The colour of your walls was dictated by your family crest, rather than your individual inclination. To overstep the mark was, in the case of Nicholas Fouquet, whose magnificent chateau at Vaux le Vicomte inspired the jealousy of Louis XIV, to risk lifetime imprisonment and political disgrace.

But as the power of absolute princes ebbed away, and even more so after the French Revolution removed that power altogether, so the possibility arose that standards of taste could be set by not just the Prince and his academy, but by the people too; and that meant that those who could afford to could, and indeed were obliged to, set their own. The modern idea that beauty might lie in the eyes of individual beholders was born.

Fashion, taste, and the modern housewife

And that created a new problem altogether, for if neither God nor the King nor his academies nor the Ancients were authorized to tell people what was beautiful and tasteful, who was? And what qualified them to do so?

The result was a plethora of advice literature like that of Elsie de Wolfe, including guides on what people should wear and how they should cook, or entertain, or talk to one another. The nineteenth century witnessed the birth of a vast industry which is still with us today – this book being only one among its many manifestations.

Charles Eastlake, in his classic of the genre of 1878, *Hints on Household Taste*, admitted that he wasn't going to be able to tell his readers how to acquire good taste. The only thing he could advise them was, rather vaguely, to be brought up in the middle classes:

The general impression seems to be, that it is the peculiar inheritance of gentle blood, and independent of all training;

that, while a young lady is devoting at school, or under a governess, so many hours a day to music, so many to languages, and so many to general science, she is all this time unconsciously forming that sense of the beautiful which we call taste.[3]

Like Le Corbusier, Eastlake saw himself as writing a manifesto against what he believed was the superficial consumerism of his time, a time in which, he wrote, 'there was no upholstery which could possibly surpass that which the most fashionable upholsterer supplied'.[4]

'When did people first adopt the monstrous notion that "the last pattern out" must be the best?' he raged.[5] Charles Eastlake, as you might have guessed, didn't approve of fashion; and he made a plea for people to furnish their homes in an 'artistic' manner, and for home furnishings to be designed in the same spirit as the finest painting or sculpture.

But he was canny enough to see that in his feminine audience, fashion was more or less inescapable. 'Unfortunately,' he admitted, 'the world of fashion is so constituted that people who move in it are obliged to conform more or less to its rules; and as no lady likes to make herself conspicuous by her dress, she may reasonably abstain from wearing what has long been out of date.'[6]

Beauty, in a modern world in which individuals are free to make their own choices, should logically be the product of individual preference – it should be art – but it was also, Eastlake saw, subject to social judgement. It still is.

Homes of distinction

A century later, writing in France, the sociologist Pierre Bourdieu made the same point, albeit in starker terms. Taste, he argued, was a weapon in class war.

Bourdieu's classic work *On Distinction: a Social Critique of the Judgement of Taste* was written in the 1970s; and looking back on it now, it seems to describe a stratified, stereotyped society, every rung of which was as slavishly addicted to 'fashion' as Eastlake's Victorian women. Bourdieu applied a cruel and a critical eye to them all. The stuffy, conservative luxury of the suburban homes of the professional *haute bourgeoisie*, he wrote, was a socioeconomic weapon they used to show off their wealth. Their poorer cousins in teaching and the arts retaliated by using their simple but tasteful homes to show off the learning and the discernment, rather than the hard cash, that they possessed. The aspirational *petite bourgeoisie*, he wrote,

> deploys prodigious energy and ingenuity in 'living beyond its means'. In the home this is done by devising 'nooks' and 'corners' (the 'kitchen corners', 'dining areas', 'bedroom corners', etc. recommended by the women's magazines) intended to multiply the rooms ... not to mention all the forms of 'imitation' and all the things that can be made to 'look like' something they are not.[7]

Meanwhile, at the bottom of the social scale, the proletariat exhibited apparent indifference to fashion or taste, preferring sentimental art and filling food.

So the distinction of Bourdieu's title was a social, rather than an artistic one; but there's one important thing upon which Eastlake and Bourdieu agreed: that while taste might seem to be personal, implicit, and apparently natural, in actual fact it is heavily conditioned.

'The ideology of natural taste,' wrote Bourdieu, 'owes its plausibility and its efficacy to the fact that, like all the ideological strategies generated in the everyday class struggle, it naturalizes real differences, converting differences in the modes of acquisition of culture into differences of nature.'[8]

Bourdieu was keenly aware of the oddness of bringing together the rarefied world of art, beauty, and aesthetic appreciation with the everyday life of the home. The study of domestic décor, he noted, was one in which 'the elaborated taste for the most refined objects is reconnected with the elementary taste for the flavours of food'.[9]

And yet it's what we do all the time. No wonder we have so many words for the ways we decorate our homes, from taste, to atmosphere, to *Stimmung*, to beauty and art themselves. We seem to work our way through every sense except the one we are actually describing.

Décor and decorum

But there's one word we haven't talked about yet, perhaps the most obvious one of all: decoration itself.

The root of the word is found in the Latin *decorum*, which, just as it does in English, means appropriateness in modes and manners. After all, to decorate a room is to dress it up for an occasion:

Dining in good taste: the interior of Elsie de Wolfe's Villa Trianon at Versailles.

Successful Dining, as Elsie de Wolfe observed, isn't only about the food, but also the setting, physical and social, in which it is eaten.

Decoration is a sort of scenery; and it always has been. The chief decorators of Louis XIV's France, like the painter Charles Le Brun, started out as scenographers for the theatre: even the great playwright Moliere held the post of the King's Upholsterer. Vitruvius complained about the theatrical dispositions and sensibilities of the painters and decorators of his time, while Mario Praz's concept of *Stimmung* was born out of adventures in the performance of music. Even Elsie de Wolfe started out as an actress before she started dining in style.

I guess that's why my parents couldn't help smiling when they saw what I'd done to my teenage bedroom. They could see I was *theatrical*. As a child, I'd made camps in my bedroom. Now I'd made my bedroom camp. I'd made the room into scenery for a performance that was never going to happen – not while I was a teenager, anyway. I was never going to dine there with Elsie de Wolfe or Marie Antoinette. I was just going to lie there on my teenage bed on my own and dream of such things. Theatres and the worlds we encounter in them are fictions, and so are homes, which we dress up and decorate for the occasions we want to happen in them.

If you're worried about your domestic taste, that may be something worth remembering. The tools of the decorator – paint, paper, light, a curtain or two, and the cunning arrangement of ornaments – are every bit as makeshift and illusory as flats and props in the theatre, and they can be changed just as quickly. It takes an afternoon to paint a wall, and a few minutes to change the wattage in a light bulb. In my opinion, we don't do it often enough.

In this chapter, we've considered approaches to domestic beauty from Pythagorean mathematics to Marxist deconstruction, Romantic atmospherics to academic disputation. If we've learned anything, it's that no one has ever been able to agree on the definition of good taste, and they never will. Beauty is as ephemeral and elusive as the means we use to make it. It doesn't actually matter. Ultimately, the reason for decorating your home isn't to create an eternal work of art, to glorify the monarch, or to go one better than the neighbours.

It's simpler than that: the purpose of decorating your house is to create scenery for the life, real or not, you'd like to live in it.

4. How to Collect a Home

Since when did owning things make you happy? The burdens of possession.

Living out of a suitcase

I'm not a child or a teenager any more. I ceased to be one when I moved away from my bedroom in my parents' house. I packed my things up and went on my way; and soon enough, home ceased to be the place I had come from, and became the stuff I was carrying with me.

There wasn't much. In those days, I could fit my things into a few bags: a suitcase of clothes, a box of books, a hi-fi, posters rolled up into a tube. That was more than twenty years ago. I couldn't do it now. In the meantime, I've just collected too much stuff. Some of what I have collected over the years has been furniture, but furniture isn't the only thing with which we fill our homes. It's the other stuff that I've accumulated – and I suspect you have too – that makes up the majority of the things we have to carry around.

Every year or so, I try to throw some of it away. Some objects whose utility is obvious, or obviously expired, are easy to get rid of; but the rest is much more difficult, and I end up hanging on to all sorts of things for no reason that I can clearly explain. I'm not talking about clothes, or kitchen utensils, or other things with easily ascribed functions. I'm talking about the things that accumulate in attics, in the second drawer down in the kitchen, on the walls of teenage bedrooms, on mantelpieces, in bookshelves and at the bottoms of handbags.

To call this stuff bric-a-brac or junk or clutter is to devalue it. To think of it as ornament is perhaps useful: extraneous, additional, unnecessary, sometimes pretty, but not always. Sometimes there's a signet ring lurking in there, an antique statuette, a Sevres vase, or a first edition. But all too often, its value is difficult to articulate. What it means, precisely, is not always clear.

Buildings and furniture and décor can be designed; but this stuff generally isn't. That is not to say that individual pieces haven't been designed by anyone; but en masse, as a collection, they are, apparently, incoherent. I have no real idea as to how I have collected most of my possessions, or why.

Take books, for example. What is the point of lining the walls of rooms with books one has either already read (and will never read again) or that one will never read? Why, when their function has expired, do we still hang on to them? Why, in the age of the Kindle and the tablet, do we collect them in the first place?

And it's not just books. I have slides I shall never look at again; cassette tapes I made as a teenager that I can no longer listen to and letters no biographer will ever read. I have, in boxes I never open, collections of tropical seashells, 78-rpm records and Beatrix Potter figurines I collected as a child. Lurking at the bottom of drawers there are pulled wisdom teeth and broken cufflinks, balls of BluTack covered in fluff, and money kept from countries I shall never visit again.

In the first chapter of this book, we started with the idea that home is a fixed point of origin. We concluded the second by considering home as a nomadic affair. In the third we thought about home as ephemeral scenery. I've spent the first half of this book extolling the idea of home as light, temporary, mobile and changeable. But if I actually go and take a look at my own home, I realize I haven't taken my own advice: I'm so weighed down by my possessions that I might as well stay where I am.

Ornaments are crime

There's something wicked about collecting. Le Corbusier decried the overcrowded homes of his own era as 'furniture stores', and exhorted his readers to 'bear in mind economy in your actions, your household management, and in your thoughts'.[1] 'Ornament is Crime' wrote Adolf Loos; and ornaments, argued Frank Lloyd Wright, were the 'bête noire of the new simplicity'. 'If you want a golden rule that will fit everything, this is it,' wrote William Morris. 'Have nothing in your houses that you do not know to be useful or believe to be beautiful.'

And collectors themselves have always been seen as morally dubious, too. Orson Welles's *Citizen Kane* surrounds himself with an endless collection of trophies, from art to buildings, priceless jewels to a beautiful wife; but the lesson of his story is that possessing none of them could make him happy; and his last word, 'Rosebud', refers to a simple toy of his childhood rather than any of the precious wonders he ever amassed in his extraordinary career.

John Pierpont Morgan, like William Randolph Hearst, and many of the American robber barons on whom Kane was based, spent millions on an encyclopaedic and indiscriminate collection of European art. He had so much that he had no idea what he possessed.

Once, on enquiring where his Michelangelo was kept, his secretary reminded him: 'this bronze bust is in your library, and faces you when sitting in your chair. It has been there about a year.'[2]

But the history of collecting reaches its climax with the mysterious and complex character of the Emperor of the Holy Roman Empire, Rudolf II, who reigned between 1576 and 1612. Even at the time, everyone thought he was odd. The Venetian ambassador noted that he never smiled, or laughed, and remarked upon his manners as 'spaniolated' – that is, as haughty and withdrawn as a Spaniard.

Most of the stories about the Emperor concerned his greed. His niece, the Archduchess of Styria, wrote: 'What he knows, he feels obliged to have.'[3] Everyone knew that the only way to engage the Emperor was to bring him gifts that were, in the words of the archduchess, 'both extraordinary and miraculous'.[4]

Rudolph kept everything, and in a catalogue that was made of his collection in 1607, there were listed 101 cabinets that contained antique medals and paintings, mandrakes and the skeleton of a basilisk, clocks and astrolabes, gems and a stuffed dodo, the horn of a unicorn, and a bowl Rudolf believed to be the Holy Grail. There were lumps of real gold and fool's gold, and bestiaries filled with images of animals that never existed. He kept it all under lock and key in his *Wunderkammer*: his cabinet of curiosity.

All sorts of rumours circulated about the Emperor, but perhaps the strangest was one that was used to explain his unprecedented avarice. The reason he had amassed so many possessions, people said, was because he hoped that among them he would find the philosopher's stone, with which his court alchemists could turn any substance into gold. He would lock himself into his *Wunderkammer* for days at a time, they would say, and sit there searching his eclectic possessions for the elusive stone.

He never found it, of course. Instead, he spent his life shut up in his cabinet, isolated from the people, the politics, and the empire he was meant to be leading; with catastrophic results for himself (he was deposed), for his collection (which was dispersed), and for his empire, which dissolved into thirty years of war after his death. If there was ever a cautionary tale about collecting, then the story of Rudolf II's *Wunderkammer* provides it.

I suspect that very few of us can claim to possess a unicorn's horn or the holy grail; but if we counted the things we have stored up in our homes, we might find that they numbered well into the thousands – as many as Rudolf II collected. Living in a modern world filled with countless objects, we are all guilty of the avarice of emperors.

We've never really approved of clutter, and we still don't. TV shows like *Get Your House in Order*, *Hoarding: Buried Alive*, or *Mission Organization* show us how to get rid of the stuff, and persuade us that the desire to collect is driven by unresolved psychological trauma. Grief for the loss of loved ones, for example, manifests itself in an inability to throw away the things they have left behind. A desire to shop masks an inner emptiness.

Each time, the process of throwing things away liberates participants from problems that have, quite literally, been weighing them down for years. Griefs are resolved, fears faced, and burdens lifted, as the objects are carried out of the house and taken to the charity shop or the skip. Imagine it happening to Rudolf II: could the Thirty Years War have been avoided if he'd gone on *Get Your House in Order*? What problems could you solve if you were able to throw everything away?

The strange comfort of things: a Renaissance cabinet of curiosities.

The comfort of things

Our possessions, and our inability to stop ourselves acquiring more of them, still present us with a problem. In 2008, the anthropologist Danny Miller wrote that we live in 'what sometimes seems like a deluge of goods and shopping. We tend to assume that this has two results: that we are more superficial, and that we are more materialistic, that our relationships to things comes at the expense of our relationships to people.'[5]

It was a hypothesis that Miller decided to test by interviewing as many of the inhabitants of a certain Stuart Street in London as would speak to him. While the street itself might have been made up of a uniform terrace of houses, he found within them as diverse a range of homes and of people as a global city at the turn of the twenty-first century could provide.

Miller found collections of CDs obsessively arranged in alphabetical order, hoards of photographs, boxes of Christmas decorations, collections of toys from McDonald's Happy Meals, greetings cards, and a population of hundreds of plastic ducks. Every house he found was a *Wunderkammer* of sorts – an obsessive collection of things neither obviously useful nor beautiful, collected seemingly at random.

Miller composed his study into a series of vignettes of the lives lived behind the closed doors of Stuart Street; and he chose to start with an account of a house belonging to a man who had no clutter at all. Perhaps such a person might, being unfettered by possessions, be free of the superficialities of modern life, and free to form relationships with people rather than things.

But Miller soon discovered that his initial hypothesis was mistaken. Aside from a carpet and some furniture, George's flat was completely empty. There were no plants, no posters, no postcards: nothing at all. 'There is a violence to such emptiness,' he reflected:

Faced with nothing, one's gaze is not returned, attention is not circumscribed. There is a loss of shape, discernment and integrity. There is no sense of the person as the other, who defines one's own boundary and extent. I was trying to concentrate on what he was saying, but I was disturbed by the sheer completeness of the void.[6]

As the interview continued, the absence of objects in George's home, Miller found, mirrored the absence of agency in his life. The reason his home was empty, free of clutter and junk, wasn't some higher state of aesthetic consciousness or spiritual freedom from desire.

George had had no career to speak of, no friends, no interests, and, after his parents had died, only one very distant relative whom he rarely saw. Miller left in tears: 'One simply couldn't escape the conclusion,' he recollected, 'that this was a man, more or less waiting for his time on earth to be over, but who at the age of seventy-six had never yet seen his life actually begin.'[7]

As he worked his way up and down Stuart Street, Miller found time and time again that the things people had collected, and the ways in which they had acquired them, seemed to mirror the ways in which they related to people, too.

Mr and Mrs Clarke filled their homes with gifts for and from extensive networks of friends and family. Marina collected toys from

McDonald's Happy Meals, Mrs Stone greetings cards, and Jacques beer glasses filched from pubs.

In each case, Miller listened as his subjects spoke about their possessions: not just to what they were saying but how they were saying it. Elia was a magical storyteller, he recalled: 'Her hands dance the tale she tells and through some sleight of hand a ghost suddenly appears and dominates the room for a while, before fading back into some furniture or piece of clothing that has its home in her world.'[8]

As he listened to her, Miller realized that, for Elia, possessions were haunted by the people who had made them or given them to her. She used the stool in the corner, for example, which had been made by her grandfather, to refer to him as if it were his presence in the room; and she encouraged her own grandchildren to play with it just as they might have played with him.[9]

And as he listened to the inhabitants of Stuart Street, Miller also looked around him, not just at the things that they had collected, but also at the ways in which they had arranged them.

For example, Mary and Hugh's copious collections of snaps, framed certificates and other documents were hung on the walls of their sitting room in groups. One section of wall related to their origins in Ireland, others to their life as landlords of various pubs around London, others again to their Catholic faith. Sitting in their sitting room, they could, from the comfort of their armchairs, remember where they had come from, survey their busy and sociable lives, and contemplate their religion.

But Miller noticed that the ways in which some people arranged their clutter seemed to contain more subtle messages. Marjorie, he observed, didn't just own a diverse array of objects, both precious and worthless, but displayed them together in all sorts of ironic couplings: serious newspaper clippings were pinned to the notice board along with silly photographs; real flowers shared vases with fake ones, and 'a white ceramic Chinese figure of Serenity' was displayed along with a farting fish.[10]

Marjorie's unexpected juxtapositions, in which one serious object was always undermined by another ridiculous one, reflected, Miller argued, her own pragmatic, humorous approach to a long life spent as a foster mother to over forty children. By the end of the study, Miller was able to conclude that collecting was not just the sign of empty avarice. 'The closer our relationships are with objects,' he wrote, 'the closer our relationships are with people.'[11]

He entitled his book *The Comfort of Things*. It might seem that the similarities Miller was spotting between human and object relationships were the inevitable, inadvertent results of the way that people made their homes. But he himself was persuaded that everyone seemed to have a personal aesthetic that governed the ways in which they related to both objects and people. This was not taste as such, but a pattern of repeated behaviours and arrangements.

Furthermore, this is something that Miller came to believe was entirely deliberate:

> Some things may be gifts or objects retained from the past, but they have decided to live with them, to place them in lines, or higgledy piggledy; they made the room minimalist or crammed to the gills. These things are not a random collection. They have been gradually accumulated as an expression of that person or household.[12]

These arrangements of things – higgledy-piggledy or in lines, en masse like the plastic ducks, or placed in contradictory collage like Marjorie's Chinese Serenity figure and her farting fish – were things that, he argued, had been carefully constructed over time.

And like the work of any artist, the ways in which people arrange things, wrote Miller, 'form the basis on which people judge the world and themselves'.[13] It's a sentence that has an echo of Bachelard's idea of home as a 'real cosmos'.[14] He was referring to the house as a building; but he could equally have been talking about the bric-a-brac it contained.

The alchemy of collecting

It has always been that way. If the rumours are to be believed, the Emperor Rudolf was convinced that somewhere in his collection he would find, one day, the philosopher's stone.

He was wrong: the philosopher's stone was not *in* his collection. Rather, it *was* his collection. The wonders and the instruments it contained were collected to record and to measure the heavens and the earth, and the court scholars who worked in it, like the astronomers Tycho Brahe and Johannes Kepler, used them to revolutionize our understanding of the world, leading to the work of Galileo, Newton and the discovery of gravity itself.

Likewise, the artworks and the curiosities he owned now form the core of the collections of several major national museums; and their creation transformed the careers and reputations of artists as diverse as Arcimboldo, famous for his portraits of the Emperor made of fruit, fish, and flowers, the watercolourist Joris Hoefnagel, and the jewellers Jan Vermeyen and Ottavio Miseroni.

Rudolph's cabinet of curiosities was the germ of the modern museum, the lab, the studio, and the archive; but like many of its contemporaries, it was not organized, catalogued, or classified according to any scientific system we would recognize. That is why we still call such places *Wunderkammer*, 'wonder-chambers': they are cabinets of curiosity provoked rather than curiosity satisfied.

The curiosities in his uncle Ferdinand's cabinet in the castle of Ambras had been grouped by material and colour. At the Residenz in Munich, those of the Elector of Bavaria had been arranged into compositions on tables by size. No one would organize an art collection or an archive that way today.

Rudolph's own collection, laid out on a green baize table in a long room, was arranged into three different sections: *naturalia*, including stuffed animals, horns, plants and minerals; *artificialia* – examples of human artifice – from jewellery to weapons; and *scientifica* – instruments of knowledge – from telescopes to books. All of creation was arranged into levels, from brute nature to higher wisdom. The *Wunderkammer* of Rudolph II was a whole world, a cosmos, structured in relationship to knowledge.

Now I'm not going to try to argue that the chaotic bookshelves in my spare bedroom or the odds and ends on my kitchen table – or yours – will ever lead to anything like the discovery of gravity or the creation of a national art museum; but, like the contents of Rudolf's *Wunderkammer* (and those of the houses in Stuart Street), they include gifts from the people I have known, books I have read, souvenirs of the places I have visited, and things I have made. Collected over years, my bric-a-brac reifies the things I have learned in a lifetime.

And in the ways in which it has been arranged, my collections reify *how* I have learned these things. My books are largely arranged by subject matter; the gifts I have received in ascending order of preciousness: the most precious kept concealed, so that I don't lose them, the most worthless thrown pell-mell into a bowl on the kitchen table. It is only I that can relegate some things to the deep storage of the attic, and it is only I who remembers what is there.

Like Rudolf's *Wunderkammer*, my stuff is classified and structured in relationship to my knowledge of the world from which it has been taken. No wonder I find it so uncomfortable to throw things away.

I'm not on my own. Think of George on Stuart Street, or those elderly people taken away from all the clutter accumulated in their homes to medicalized 'homes'. All too many quickly lose their minds, however physically comfortable their new accommodation might be. Unlike the furniture with which we equip our homes, or the buildings with which we shelter them, the objects with which we clutter them – the things of 'sentimental value' we accumulate over a lifetime – solidify our memory and our knowledge of the world. Without these things to anchor them, our apprehensions slip away.

Keep learning, keep collecting

Whatever Renaissance moralists or modern architects and designers might say, ornaments, bric-a-brac, clutter, call it what you will, are not necessarily a crime. Our homes are little worlds, arranged from fragmentary pieces of the larger one beyond them. As we learn more, as we build those little worlds, we map their geographies, tell their histories, and elucidate their scientific laws. But the more we learn about them as we build our homes, the more we build not just a little world, but a geography, a history, a science of ourselves.

And science itself, invented in the vaulted cellars of Rudolf II's *Wunderkammer*, posits that the world, and our knowledge of it, are always incomplete, and always will be. On the one hand, new stars, microbes and elements will always be there to be discovered. On the other, each new discovery causes us to reinterpret and to reclassify what we already know. If collecting is a science of the self, then you should never stop collecting clutter; you should never stop sorting through its protean jumble; and you should never stop throwing junk away.

I, for one, hope that I do not already know everything I will ever know. I hope we all still have things to learn. In the twenty-five years since I left home I have amassed thousands of objects; and in the process of amassing them, their meaning has changed. Once I acquired a CD player, for example, my cassette tapes left my audio collection and joined, along with the 78-rpm records, my antiques collection. Now I have a Kindle, the same is happening to my library.

Conversely, I have thrown away things that were once very precious to me: the posters with which I decorated the walls of my student bedroom, for example, or the silver cushions with which I ornamented my teenage boudoir. They have gone to the rubbish collection, their use and their meaning long since expired.

What we collect around us reifies what we know and how we know it; but knowledge itself is dynamic. When we build a house, we remember where we have come from. When we furnish a home, we play with who we could be. When we decorate a room, we imagine the life we would like to live in it. When we collect and arrange, and recollect and rearrange, its contents, we discover, again and again, who we are.

5. How to Keep a Home

Welcome to domestic bliss.

My Saturday mornings

Joan Rivers put it best: 'I hate housework! You make the beds, you do the dishes and six months later you have to start all over again.'[1] I know what she means.

So far, this book has asked you to think about how to build a home, how to arrange the furniture that it contains, how to decorate it, and how to collect the objects that will fill it. Do all of those things, you might be forgiven for thinking, and you have made yourself a home. Your work, you might imagine, is done.

Your work is just beginning; and the beds and dishes are just the tip of the iceberg. There's the drying up, too, and the putting it all away. Then there's all that wiping down, hoovering, dusting and polishing. There's the cleaning out the back of the fridge, and the scrubbing down the inside of the oven. There's window cleaning to do; and there's the perennial decluttering and rearranging.

And then there's redecorating, repainting and replastering ceilings and walls, sometimes knocking them down, or building new ones. There are repairs to roofs after storms or snow, rewiring, replumbing, and the plugging of leaks. There's the mortgage to be rearranged, or the phone, TV or Wi-Fi contract to be sorted or the council tax to be paid (all of which seem to involve interminable hours on the telephone).

And we haven't even started on the garden.

You will not be paid for undertaking any of this work, and it will not contribute to your continuing personal and professional development. It will not end up on your curriculum vitae or lead to a promotion. And what is more, this work will be endless and, unless you are consigned to a care home, or have the means to live in an hotel, it will haunt you until the end of your days, becoming more and more difficult with every year.

As Miss Rivers observed, this work will never be finished. Do the washing up, and you know that, six months later, you will have to do it all over again. Hoover the floor and the fluff will reappear in seconds. Wipe the surfaces and someone will spill something on them in moments. The fridge will continue to go mouldy, and the oven greasy for as long as you use them. Clean the windows, and the dirty rain will fall on them the next day. Roofs will leak, walls will always need to be repainted, and the garden will keep on growing in all sorts of ways you never imagined.

And all these hours of unpaid work will be undertaken in your downtime. For me, it's Saturday mornings, when I should be lying in bed with a hangover. And what's worse is that all of it, all of this work that I shouldn't have to be doing, is taking place in the one place I shouldn't have to be doing work at all: in fact, the one place I come to in order to get away from work. It is taking place at home.

Separate spheres?

It wasn't always so. Before the nineteenth century, work wasn't something you went to (or came home from). Work was what, and who, you were. Being a king, or priest, or merchant or a peasant weren't jobs: they were rungs on the great ladder of being, castes, estates that governed who you could marry, what you could wear, where you could go, whether you could read, or eat.

And where you could live, for the places in which people lived and worked were one and the same. Castles or palaces weren't the places to which a prince returned after a hard day princing somewhere else: they were the manifestation of his status, and, in the case of castles, the very real guarantee of his own personal security and power. You weren't a monk unless you lived in a monastery; and merchants lived above the shop. In Renaissance Florence, banking families like the Medici and Strozzi and Pazzi lived, literally, on top of the money deposited in their banks. The houses of seventeenth-century Amsterdam were essentially habitable warehouses, supplied by the network of canals that linked them to the seaborne empire beyond. In cottages everywhere, peasant families have always lived with their livestock and their agricultural implements. There is no fairytale in which some goodwife is not hard at work stirring pottage or porridge, spinning by the fire, sweeping the grate, cleaning the table, or milking the cow.

But in the nineteenth century, with the advent of the Industrial Revolution, work began to become something that took place outside the home. For the governing classes, it was concentrated in ministries and chancellories; for the bourgeoisie in offices and exchanges; for the proletariat the peasantry had become, in the factory, the plantation, and the mine. Cities themselves divided in two: into 'downtown', the 'CBD', or the bazaar, in which work was meant to happen; and the suburbs or cantonments, with their villas, lawns, and tennis clubs, from which work was apparently entirely absent.

And homes began to divide, too. Once upon a time, home had been a hall, a single room in which all of life, work and play had been promiscuously mixed; but in the nineteenth century new rooms were invented: parlours for talking in, drawing rooms for withdrawing to, sitting rooms for sitting in, playrooms for playing in. The kitchens and sculleries and laundries in which work was meant to happen were hidden out of sight in basements, or out the back.

All those drawing rooms and parlours were decorated by women for women, to sit and talk in while their men were at work, earning the money to pay for them. That's certainly what Charles Eastlake thought as he addressed his *Hints on Household Taste* to the wives of the bourgeoisie, or Elsie de Wolfe instructed them about successful dining. The division of cities, buildings and rooms into separate spheres marked a division between the genders;[2] and the world had been divided in two: between those who worked, and those who didn't.

A woman's work is never done

Pay those ladies a call, however, ask them what they were up to, and you might have been given a very different picture.

No one bears better witness to just how much labour the nineteenth-century home could actually be for women than Mrs Beeton. Her famous *Book of Household Management* was, like *Hints on Household Taste*, addressed to aspirational Victorian housewives; but while Eastlake imagined well-bred ladies following fashion at their leisure, Mrs Beeton saw them hard at work.

Being a housewife meant being up before anyone else (with, naturally, a cold or tepid bath for the health), stoking the range and preparing breakfast, mending clothes in the morning before making social calls of no more than fifteen minutes at a time before lunch, managing servants, attending to the health of children, organizing entertainments for the evening, and, when everyone else had gone to bed, getting down to work, breaking lump sugar, stoning raisins, washing and drying currants:

> The evening, too, is the best time for setting right her account
> for the expenditure and duly writing a statement of moneys
> received and paid and also for making memoranda of any art-
> icles she may require for her storeroom or other departments.[3]

If it makes the housewife sound a little like a businesswoman as well as a skivvy, then that was entirely deliberate. The injunction with which Mrs Beeton begins her book is chilling: 'As with the commander of an army,' she wrote, 'or the leader of any enterprise, so is it with the mistress of a house.'[4]

Social visits formed part of a currency: 'A strict account,' she wrote, should be kept of ceremonial visits, and notice how soon your visits have been returned.'[5] Even solitary leisure was subjected to the laws of progress and productivity: 'intended to the mind,' she enjoined, 'as whetting is to the scythe to sharpen the edge of it, which would otherwise grow dull and blunt.'[6]

Mrs Beeton's *Book of Household Management* is an account against which ideas of the home as a refuge from the world of work starts to look like a rather partial view, written by men who never had to do any housework, wealthy enough to be unable to imagine that their womenfolk wouldn't have servants to do their housework for them.

But home wasn't a refuge from work for most women, it *was* work. What is more, subjected as it was by a Mrs Beeton to minute accountancy, strict time management, and rigid standards of quality control, it wasn't so different from all those jobs in the office or the factory or the ministry after all.

The domestic industrial revolution

Mrs Beeton imagined the home not as a refuge from the factory, but as a sort of factory in itself, churning out endless meals, clothes, social occasions, comforts, children and all the rest of it. Since that time, the home has been subjected to the same processes of mechanization as the world of work. In Mrs Beeton's day that factory might have been crowded by washerwomen, scullery maids, cooks, and messenger boys. A century and a half later, they have been replaced by washing machines, dishwashers, and microwaves. Your kitchen, and mine, are among the most heavily technologized spaces on the planet.

It's a revolution that has taken place over a century of struggle between the sexes. Take something innocent sounding, for example: the 'kitchen triangle': the pattern made as you move between fridge, sink, and cooker while you're cooking. Speak to anyone in a kitchen showroom and they'll tell you it should be as small as possible. It's conventional wisdom, now.

But it hasn't always been. The kitchen triangle is the result of the same sort of ergonomic studies that drive the design of cars in factories, or the extraction of bauxite from mines. The time-and-motion study techniques used by Henry Ford, for example, were used in the 1920s by designers like Margarete Schütte-Lihotzky, working on social housing in Frankfurt. Schütte-Lihotzky proudly claimed she'd never cooked a meal in her life, but she spent weeks watching what other women did in the kitchen as they prepared dinner for their families.

She did it to set them free; and many feminists of her time, borrowing insights from the processes of mass production, campaigned to have housework outsourced from the home. They proposed mass dining clubs, kindergartens, public laundries and washing facilities where they could leave the duties of the home and go out, like their menfolk, to earn money. Occasionally their revolutionary campaigns bore fruit in reality, especially in the fervid atmosphere of Russia in the 1920s. The Narkomfin apartment building in Moscow, for example, was designed as a revolutionary 'social condenser', with communal kitchens on the ground floor completely separate from fifty-four sleeping units upstairs.

Just like men before them, women were convinced that the machine would set them free. In 1912 Christine Frederick, a housewife herself, campaigned for a 'new housekeeping'[7] in homes designed on industrial principles:

I turned eagerly to my husband. 'George,' said I, 'that efficiency gospel is going to mean a lot to modern housekeeping, in spite of the doubts I have. Do you know I am going to work out those principles here in our home! I won't have you men doing all the great and noble things! I'm going to find out how those experts conduct investigations, and all about it, and then apply it to my factory, my business, my home.'[8]

But is housework work?

Home isn't the opposite of work; and it never has been. There is, however, one fundamental difference between the work that takes place at home and the work that takes place outside it. Housework isn't paid work.

In 1972, the activist Selma James launched the international campaign 'Wages for Housework'. The problem that vexed James wasn't money per se, or the lack of independence caused by its absence, or even the men who imposed this drudgery on 'their' women. It was that housework was, quite simply, not understood as work. Interviewed recently in the *Guardian*, James says:

> By demanding payment for housework we attack what is terrible about caring in our capitalist society, while protecting what is great about it, and what it could be. We refuse housework, because we think everyone should be doing it.[9]

For quite aside from the very real consequences of not getting paid for work – slavery and poverty and low status – the strange nature of housework raised another question: if it wasn't paid work, then what sort of work was it?

The problem is that however much we try to technologize it, monetize it, politicize it, or account for it – however hard we work at making it work – housework just doesn't seem to conform to capitalist (or Marxist) models of labour. That is, it is not a trade-off between time or effort, and money. It can't be. Even Selma James admitted that 'this work is not like other work: we hate it, and we want to do it'.[10]

In fact, housework may be more similar to those types of work that predated the Industrial Revolution. When the sociologist Paul J. J. Pennartz asked one of his interviewees, a Dutch housewife, why she couldn't leave the washing up undone before sitting down to dinner, she replied:

> I get nervous while eating, I can't stand it . . . I like to relax
> while I am eating, I don't taste the food when everything is in
> a mess . . . because I feel haunted by the work waiting for me.[11]

We might all confess to being haunted by work, or internalizing its demands and strictures, but at least we get to come home from it. For housewives, however, there is no going home. They are there already; and they are at work all the time. Rather like the prince or the priest or the merchant or the peasant of the olden days, they *are* their work.

There's something else that's particularly unmodern about housework, and the people who do it. It's something Joan Rivers was thinking about when she complained about doing the dishes: the trouble with housework isn't just that you have to do it, it's that you have to do it over and over again. Most housework isn't about

What does the Industrial Revolution look like when it's at home?

o back *from Electricity* oned cooking now!"

rs have thermostat control on the oven,
boiling plates, and new, variable switches
fect heat-control from fast boiling to slow
d lower, if you want it!

Go round and see one at your Electricity Service Centre.
They are friendly, knowledgeable people there, and will
be glad to help you. They can also let you have details
about easy payments, and the new, free book, full of
clever ideas for saving work, ELECTRICITY IN YOUR
KITCHEN: or you are welcome to write for a copy to
EDA, 2 Savoy Hill, London, W.C.2.

ELECTRICITY
a Power of Good
for cooking!
AND FOR WATER-HEATING TOO!

improving things. It's the endless, thankless, repetitive drudgery of keeping them pretty much the same.

And that is not something we are trained to value. The modern conception of the 'career' is deeply wedded to the idea of progress. Teachers hope their pupils will advance through school, businessmen that their businesses will grow, farmers that their crops will multiply, doctors that new diseases will be cured, and administrators that quality will be enhanced as well as assured. When did you last hear anyone at work sing the praises of keeping things as they are?

Whether you're a Marxist or a neoliberal, a biological evolutionist or a born-again Christian, history is told as a story of improvement – technological, social, scientific, moral – from slavery to Communism or the victory of the markets, from the amoeba to Superman, from analogue to digital, Creation to the Rapture. Modernity itself is an idea based on the assumption that time moves forward, and that things get better.

But when it comes to fixing leaks or taking the bins out it doesn't feel like we are moving forward. At home, the progressive law of materialist dialectics is well and truly cancelled out by the rather less thrilling second law of thermodynamics. Making a home isn't really about making things better. It's more about stopping them getting worse. No wonder we all try to get out of it.

Drudgerie divine

But perhaps we shouldn't. After all, that dirty kitchen floor isn't going to mop itself. Mrs Beeton was adamant that housework lent real value to the woman who undertook it:

She ought always to remember that she is the first and the last, the alpha and the omega in the whole government of her establishment, that it is by her conduct that its whole internal policy is regulated. She is, therefore, a person of far more importance in a community than she usually thinks she is.[12]

But housework is not just about status. It is worth considering, for an (unpaid) moment, that there are some things worth doing even if we aren't given money for doing them.

Paul Pennartz's sociological investigations of the home led him to some unexpected conclusions about the value of housework. His study started by asking participants 'When is it most pleasant at home?' and, not unexpectedly, people cited times like getting in from work, or sleeping in on Sunday morning, or sitting in front of the telly, or around the dinner table: times that involved being together with nearest and dearest, at leisure.

But when he asked the question 'When is it least pleasant at home?' he didn't get the converse answer. One mother and house-wife reacted by saying:

Some days I'm depressed . . . I think in the afternoon . . . because in the morning I'm busy with housework . . . But in the afternoon, yes, for a few hours . . . from about one to four o'clock . . . at three o'clock I start cooking again.[13]

It wasn't being busy with housework in the morning she found depressing, but the aimless afternoon, with no work to do. Given the option of lying on the sofa, undisturbed, eating chocolates, she'd rather not. Which suggests that there are other definitions of work, and its value, than the old capitalist or Marxist one of the selling of time, attention and effort for money.

I currently have a student, Kate Lampitt Adey, who is interviewing women who knit in their leisure time.[14] They don't do it because they expect to make money, they tell her, or because they want to make great works of textile art. These women aren't professional crafts-people or politicized yarn-bombers, who cover public monuments in their knitting as a form of feminist protest. Quite simply, they can't stand having idle hands; and they like making things for the sake of making them. Some of them enjoy the process of making things so much that they often unravel what they have made so that they can make it all over again.

Kate compares this sort of knitting to 'serious leisure'. It's a concept coined in 1992 by the sociologist Robert Stebbins, who studied how we often turn the activities we undertake in our free time into a sort of challenge or work, be it learning how to play a musical instrument or to ski, or building muscles in the gym. Like housework, or knitting, such activities aren't motivated by the prospect of payment but are things – sometimes difficult and exhausting things – we undertake for their own sake.

Serious leisure activities can be an expensive and difficult business. They are often what we take time off work to do: to visit historic sites, dutifully photographing the monuments; to go to foreign countries to wander round the art galleries, ticking off the local delicacies or even to lie on a beach *working* on the tan; to visit the health spa to lose, or learn to lift, a specified weight. All too often, in what we define as our leisure time, we subject ourselves to the same rules of measurement, productivity and progress as we do in our hours of wage-slavery. But at least we might learn something, or lose a pound or two, or get better at skiing or playing an instrument, or knitting. It would be difficult to say the same about housework.

Now, Kate is interested in why the women she is interviewing are so reluctant to finish their knitting; and she's realized that, rather than the product, it is the psychological state induced by the process of knitting that they really enjoy – what she calls 'flow'.

Coined by the psychologist Mihaly Csikszentmihalyi, flow is a way of thinking about work that has nothing to do with money, or career, or status, or even, necessarily, producing anything very interesting. In fact, it's not really about what you're doing at all. It's about the way you're doing it. 'The ego falls away. Time flies. Every action, movement and thought follows inevitably from the previous one, like playing jazz.'[15]

There are several criteria for the sort of work that can achieve flow: clear, attainable, but challenging physical goals, and apparently uninterrupted time. Flow is something we seek in all manner of the activities we might undertake in our leisure time, from running, or skiing, or sailing, to playing an instrument, or singing in a band, or meditating, or doing yoga.

All of them require concentration and energy, but don't really rely on a result. 'Flow' activities are ones Csikszentmihalyi calls 'autotelic': that is, they serve no end other than themselves. You don't do them for money, or promotion, or recognition, but because you have to.

Csikszentmihalyi was talking about composing symphonies, playing sport, performing in a jazz band, or meditation; but he could have been discussing doing the dishes. It, too, is an 'autotelic' activity that goes nowhere, produces, apparently, nothing new, and makes no money.

I'm not arguing that housework is intrinsically interesting (or that anything is), or occupies the same cultural status as playing jazz (although it's considerably more important). Rather, I'm arguing that housework, repetitive and endless as it is, is something that could, with the right attitude, induce a state of flow.

I'm not really saying anything new. In seventeenth-century England, the Anglican vicar and poet George Herbert wrote a hymn we still sing today, that contains a curious verse:

> All may of Thee partake:
> Nothing can be so mean,
> Which with his tincture – 'for Thy sake' –
> Will not grow bright and clean.

> A servant with this clause
> Makes drudgerie divine:
> Who sweeps a room as for Thy laws,
> Makes that and th' action fine.

> This is the famous stone
> That turneth all to gold;
> For that which God doth touch and own
> Cannot for less be told.[16]

We don't value housework, but perhaps we should. It's not something we're going to be able to get out of doing any time soon.

Make time for mopping

When we talk about home as a refuge from the world, we often imagine the barricades we'll need to build to defend it will be made of architecture, furniture, wallpaper, bibelots and so on. We've already seen how unreliable they can be.

Imagine if that barricade was made not of objects, and did not enclose a space.

Imagine if, instead, it was made of activities, and enclosed a time – a different sort of time to the one that is measured and alarmed on iPhones and laptops, paid for by the hour or the month, pegged against improved productivity targets, and tied to visions for enhancement. Imagine it enclosed a time where progress did not happen, in which nothing was paid for, and the minutes passed by unnoticed. Imagine it was a time of flow. Imagine if you could have that time without going anywhere or paying anyone. Imagine if you could make it your own for free.

It's closer to home than you think. Housework creates nothing new, and leaves us back where we started. It creates time out of time. Making yourself at home does not come out of following fashions, accumulating more objects or better furniture, or making bigger buildings. It comes out of the act of keeping a home.

You asked me how to make yourself at home. Now, walk to the cupboard under the stairs, and take out that mop. Do it again tomorrow. You're already there.

6. How to Make a Home When You're Not at Home

How to make yourself at home when you've got no home: tramps asleep on the
Embankment, London, 1930s.

Home alone?

Where are you reading this? Are you nestled on a sofa in front of the fire? Are you perched at the kitchen table? Are you in bed? Are you in a garden, in the sun? Or are you in the bath? As you read this, are you at home, on your own? As I write it, am I?

In this book we've explored several different ways of making oneself at home. We've looked at building homes, furnishing them, decorating them, collecting them, and keeping them. We started with the idea that home should mean a secure, ordered, beautiful and personal refuge from the world. Along the way we have discovered that home can be insecure, disorderly, ugly, impersonal, and hard work.

But imagine if your home was taken away. You would miss something. What would you miss the most? The cooking and the cleaning? Your bric-a-brac? The tasteful surroundings? The comfortable furniture? The building you live in? I suspect it would be none of these things per se but, rather, the very sense of quiet refuge that a child's drawing of a house brings to mind. If there's one thing we assume about home it is that it must be private.

'The house protects the dreamer,' wrote Gaston Bachelard, 'the house allows one to dream in peace,'[1] for after all, it is when we are asleep, unconscious to threat, that we are at our most vulnerable. All the paraphernalia of home, from a protective roof to the miniature stockades of furniture and objects, from calming décor to an orderly sense of hygiene, are there to protect us as we dream, by sheltering us as we sleep.

The assumption that the home must provide privacy is one that has underpinned most of the ideal homes in this book, from Bachelard's turreted dreamhouse to the glazed bathroom of Le Corbusier's machine for living in (presumably not overlooked by neighbours); from Mario Praz's resonance chambers of the soul to the treasure houses of Danny Miller to the ordered domestic enterprise of Mrs Beeton. In all of them, the house and the self are imagined as one.

Down and out in 1984

If you want to understand just how fundamental privacy is to our concept of home, it's worth reading George Orwell's dystopian novel *1984*. The story begins with our antihero, Winston Smith, hunting around his apartment for a spot in which he can escape the all-seeing electronic eye of Big Brother, brought into his home via a prophetic version of the television that could both receive and transmit images:

> There was of course no way of knowing whether you were being watched at any given moment. How often, or on what system, the Thought Police plugged in on any individual wire was guesswork. It was even conceivable that they watched

everybody all the time. But at any rate they could plug in your wire whenever they wanted to. You had to live – did live, from habit that became instinct – in the assumption that every sound you made was overheard, and, except in darkness, every movement scrutinized.[2]

The point is a simple but chilling one: you can have a house, you can furnish it with whatever you like, and fill it with anything you fancy; you can paint the walls any colour you want, and keep it as messy as you desire, but if it's not private, you won't really be able to make yourself at home there.

Orwell knew from personal experience what it was like to live without privacy. In 1933 he spent several months *Down and Out in Paris and London.* In Paris, he worked as a *plongeur*, washing up in the restaurant of a luxury hotel. In London, he lived on the street, sleeping in hostels at night, and wandering the city aimlessly by day. There were many disadvantages, he discovered, about being down and out, but chief among them was the lack of any sense of privacy: his friend Paddy, another London tramp, described vividly an attempt to sleep on the street itself:

You got to be on your bench by eight o'clock, because dere ain't too many benches and sometimes dey're all taken. And you got to try to get to sleep at once. 'Tis too cold to sleep much after twelve o'clock, an' de police turns you off at four in de mornin'. It ain't easy to sleep, dough, wid dem bloody trams flyin' past your head all de time, an' dem sky-signs across de river flickin' on an' off in your eyes.[3]

It was only when he terminated his experience as a tramp, and returned to a state of privacy, that Orwell realized what he'd been missing.

Privacy is a privilege

In all the homes we've rummaged through in this book, there have been people who have had privacy and people who have not. Mrs Beeton's servants would not have had rooms of their own; and in the elegant chateaux of *Ancien Régime* France, footmen were expected to sleep at the foot of their masters' curtained beds. The *Wunderkammer* was a private space kept tightly under the prince's lock and key: everyone else milled around in the great hall, or sat together around the fire in their one-room huts.

Privacy has always been a scarce and costly resource, and for millions of us, it is still an unaffordable luxury. You might be sharing a single room with your whole family in a tiny tenement or crammed into a one-room hut in Nairobi, or Mumbai, where Kibera and Dharavi, with populations of 2,000 and 5,000 per hectare respectively, form the most crowded concentrations of humankind on the planet.

You might be a maid or a driver in domestic service, looking after someone else's house to earn enough to keep your own. Like Mrs Beeton's dutiful domestics, you will rise before your mistress, and your time will be subjected to her whim. While you tend her home, yours will be a small cupboard hidden round the back of the kitchen.

You may be a construction worker in the Gulf, a factory operative in China, or a migrant farm worker in England. You will sleep in a dormitory, segregated by sex, woken by a bell, dressed in identical uniforms, fed breakfast in a canteen, and bussed to work on a job you never get paid quite enough to leave.

Perhaps you never made it to the dorm. You might be lying there, reading this, on the street. You are reading, perhaps, because you know it will be dangerous to go to sleep in public, or to keep your patch next to the ventilator blowing warm air out onto the pavement from some hotel or office building.

There are millions of us who have to learn how to make ourselves at home without having a home.

The architect Mark Pimlott has recorded the ways in which people inhabit the subways that run underneath Toronto in Canada.[4] These are vast, endless interiors, but people have found ways of using the microgeographies within them to make themselves at home. They lay out toys or sunglasses or woolly hats for sale on sheets that can readily be bundled up and hurried away, on passageways where they know they'll get a good view of the approaching police. They know how to corner corners for sleeping in that will be out of sight of the security cameras.

It's an endless war of attrition. Over the past two decades writers like Mike Davies have recorded all the weapons the authorities use to keep the homeless from finding a home: from seats at bus stops that are too narrow to lie on without falling off, to medieval-looking spikes built into pavement.[5] All it means, of course, is that people have to become more and more ingenious in beating the system at its own game.

In Bangkok in Thailand a recent study by the interior designer Nuttinee Karnchanaporn has brought to light an invisible zone, 150 centimetres wide, that runs in front of the buildings on most streets. This zone is neither public space nor is it private, for while it belongs to the owners of the buildings behind it, it may not be built upon. That is, this ambiguous zone may not be built upon permanently.

But there is nothing to say that is may not be occupied temporarily; and so, each day, from nine in the morning until, say, six in the evening, it is used as a shop front, on which plastic buckets, motorcycle parts, underpants and socks, or handbags are stacked up on display. At 6 p.m. the shopkeepers clear them away and roll down their shutters; and a new set of people arrives, with plastic seats and tables, braziers, torches, and the smells and noises of street food. By midnight, these too have disappeared, and a new set of people have spread out their mats on the step, to lay down to sleep. At 6 a.m. the next day, they roll up their mats, and the cycle begins again. They will be back again the next day.

Living on the street isn't some evil aberration of city life, as many leftwing economists argue it to be. It *is* city life. Rightwing economists talk about the trickle-down effect, but any citizen of any developing city will tell you the reverse happens too: wealth trickles up from the informal microeconomies of slum, bazaar and favela to the mall, the apartment complex and the art gallery; and the two worlds are interdependent. Often, those who have had to make themselves a home without having one have been viewed as the city's problem, but in many places, they are its economic bedrock. Often people have argued that they should be tidied away, out of sight and out of mind; but of all the inhabitants of cities, they have the right, and the need, to be treated as its citizens. What is more, they have a great deal to teach the rest of us about how to live in them.

What's so good about privacy anyway?

A few years ago, I was reading a book about economic development in the Third World whose title I can no longer remember. All I recall is an image that particularly struck me. It was a photograph showing five children asleep in a bed in a one-bedroom hut. Under the photograph was a caption: 'Soon,' it said, 'we will be able to make this a thing of the past.' Under this caption was another caption: 'Which of these is more obscene: the scene in the photograph, or the caption?'

After all, what is so good about being on one's own in the first place?

After the Second World War, the slums of London's East End were cleared, and their inhabitants moved out to new, detached homes in new towns and suburbs. They were given homes of which they could only previously have dreamt: stout brick houses, with gardens and gates; modern utility furniture; labour-saving kitchens, and all the rest of it. The move was heralded as one of the great leaps forward of postwar social democracy.

In 1957, Michael Young and Peter Willmott, two of the sociologists who had been involved in this rehousing project, published a study of what had happened, comparing lives in one of the new towns in Essex with those of the people they had left behind in London.

Entitled *Family and Kinship in East London*,[6] their publication didn't come up with the answer the authorities had been hoping for.

Far from praising the order, the convenience, and the privacy of their new homes, the tenants of the new towns complained of one thing above all: loneliness. They had been brought up on the street, in and out of one another's houses, sharing everything, living in public. Now all of that had been taken away, and they – particularly women, left alone in their spacious, stout, semi-detached houses during the day – felt isolated.

It's a story that has been told time and time again. We have lived for so long with the association between privacy and privilege that we have grown to assume that being separated from other people is a universal, desirable and necessary good; but just as often, studies have shown that people would rather put up with the inconvenience of being together, rather than luxuriate in being alone.

It's not just an issue for the poor. We have been living, over the last twenty years or so, in an unprecedented and, to be frank, unanticipated revival of public life. Not only do the majority of people in the world now live in cities; those cities themselves – or at least the ways in which we imagine them – have transformed completely.

Ask someone in the 1960s what the ideal home and the ideal city would be, and it would most likely have been a prairie house in Frank Lloyd Wright's leafy suburb of Oak Park: a landscape of suburban homes, set amid quiet greensward, within easy driving distance of the mall, the country club, and the business park. The digital revolution, it was widely predicted, would complete this utopia. There would be no need for cities any more if we could all stay in touch online. There would be no need for shops any more, since everything could be purchased on the computer. In fact, by 2015, none of us would need to go out in public at all.

But it didn't happen, and now the sign of success is as likely to be a loft in Tribeca, or a house in Knightsbridge, or a flat on top of a shopping mall in Bandra as it is to be a country pile on the golf course. The most expensive house in the world, belonging to Mukesh Ambani, the world's fourth richest man, isn't a palace in a park. It's a thirty storey tower in the centre of Mumbai. The first six floors are, apparently, devoted to that perennial urban problem, parking. There are, reputedly, 600 staff, three helipads, and a health centre. A private home in any commonly understood sense of the word this is not.

New urban homes are no longer designed for the cosy verities of 1950s family life. Very often, Manhattan apartments are designed without kitchens, for example. It is assumed that you'll be eating out every day. Why cook, after all, when hundreds of Michelin-starred chefs could do it for you, in any cuisine you could desire?

Beyond the front door, be it sipping a coffee in the Piazza San Marco in Venice, or cruising the strip in Vegas, or joining the crowds at the Ganesh Chaturthi in Mumbai, people are, despite the car, despite the internet, coming together – not just to drink coffee, or eat, or work, or look at art; but to watch the people go by, to join a crowd, to be in public, in and of itself.

Once upon a time, the street was merely the way home and the only people who lingered there were those who couldn't afford to go anywhere else. Things have changed. We are all down and out in Paris and London now, and everywhere else, and what is more, we have chosen to be.

We're all living under the eye of Big Brother, too. The digital revolution seemed to promise that we could cocoon ourselves away from the public sphere; but it has in fact had the reverse effect. Mobile

Big Sister Is Watching You: domestic surveillance before the internet.

computing, ubiquitous broadband and our obsession with social media have all ensured that the public realm intrudes into the private inner sanctums of home all of the time.

As we withdraw to our drawing rooms after dinner, TV screens present us with the latest atrocity, natural disaster, or cultural spectacle. We've already broadcast our meal on Instagram, shared who we are eating with on Facebook, and what we think about it (in a well turned 140-character apophthegm) on Twitter.

And that's just the broadcasting we're doing on purpose. At the same time, our phones are pushing out data about our domestic lives that we generate inadvertently. The supermarket store-card informs the supermarket about the contents of our fridge; and the modem the media company about what we're looking at and who we are speaking to.

It all makes Orwell's Big Brother, and the CIA and KGB and MI5 and Stasi on which it was based, seem rather quaint and amateurish. It's not just the homeless, the poor, the disadvantaged who make homes without privacy these days: it's all of us. Perhaps those millions of people out there on the street can teach us something we need to know.

Being at home in public

I asked if you were at home, alone, as you were reading this, and for you to ask yourselves whether I was, too, as I wrote.

I'm not, and neither, I suspect, are you.

More likely, we are sitting in a cafe, or standing in a queue. I have written sections of this book with my laptop perched on my knees as I wait for a haircut in the barber, at a table on the train, and in a public library. How, then, when I have to write, or when you pick up the book to read, do we make ourselves at home?

Making a home might involve the ways in which people learn how to live together in flats or tenements, or dormitories in buildings old or new, borrowed or bought, rubbing away the sharp corners of masonry left behind by the previous generations for whom these structures were designed.

Home might be found in the ways in which we rearrange the chairs, or pull together the tables in a restaurant to accommodate an unexpected guest, or in the old sofa we pick up from a skip on the pavement, and carry into our new and empty home.

It might be made of scenery we don't even need to create: a certain walk through the city to work, or a seat in the park in the sun, just before the shadows slide round in the afternoon. It might be about finding a spot in the street where there's free Wi-Fi.

Or it might involve the old trick of carrying home with you: putting the family photos on the desk at work, the girlie calendar on the workshop wall, or the furry dice in the windscreen, or the way in which, like an elderly couple on the train, we spread a picnic on the table.

It might be about wiping a table in a cafe as we sit down, or clearing the snow on the pavement in front of your front door, helping to repair your neighbour's fence, or throwing a piece of litter in the bin as you walk by.

It might be something even less tangible. Undertaking research into domestic lives in Glasgow in the 1980s, the anthropologists Moira Munro and Ruth Madigan found that housewives enjoyed little more privacy than the tramps of Orwell's London, the street people of Karnchanaporn's Bangkok or Pimlott's Toronto.

After all, they were living in houses that belonged to other people: financially, usually, to their husbands, socially to their children. What was to Dad and the kids a place of relaxation was to the women who looked after it all day a place of work. Although they were at home, they were not, as we understand it, at home.

And yet these women, Munro and Madigan found, had found ways to make themselves spaces that were private, even in rooms full of people:

> They accepted other people's choice of television programme because they were only half watching, while cooking or doing the ironing. They could distance themselves from a conversation . . . by engaging with small domestic tasks . . . this 'busyness' creates a space, without the very pointed separation that would be indicated by deliberately leaving the room.[7]

They created, quietly and subtly, a bubble of privacy around them that could appear and disappear in seconds, in time.

George Orwell's friend Paddy knew he had to be on the benches of the Embankment early if he was going to get a night's sleep. The homeless who occupy the subways in Toronto know that they will be moved on by the police – and, indeed, the strategy of the police is to move them on to prevent their footholds becoming customary or in any way permanent. The inhabitants of the 150-centimetre city of Bangkok share what passes for their homes with restaurants, shopfronts and passers-by: just not at the same time.

For a long time the idea of home has been burdened with the notion of privacy. Nowadays, however, not only is this an impossible, unaffordable ideal for many, it is also the denial of an opportunity: to connect with the people around us. That is not to say that privacy is neither necessary nor possible, only to point out that perhaps we could more productively look for it at particular *times*, rather than searching for it in places like isolated suburbs, detached houses, and rooms with locks on the doors.

Home is not necessarily made of bricks and mortar, nor of furniture or other possessions, nor cushions or curtains. It is not a place or a thing. Home is a sensibility, a state of mind peculiar to each of us, something we must make for ourselves in the moments we can.

Conclusion:
How to Make a Home

We started this journey with a story. You'll remember what happened. There was a man who, despite owning everything, did not possess that one thing that anyone who has everything should rightly possess in order to be happy: a beautiful home.

You'll remember what happened. He asked for advice. He hired an architect, and the architect built him a house which was perfect, and in which every room

> was a symphony of colour, complete in itself. Walls, furniture, and fabrics harmonized in a subtle manner. Each article had its place and formed the most marvellous combinations with the others. The architect had not forgotten the least thing. Ashtrays, cutlery, candlesnuffers – he had composed everything, but everything. And it wasn't just common or garden ornament, every form, every nail expressed the individuality of its owner.[1]

And we started our exploration about how to make a home with the same assumption – it's a natural one to make in a book of domestic advice – that somehow, you can make your home better. Perfect, even.

We started with the building that must surely house any home – the house itself – and considered how, as Gaston Bachelard put it: the house we were born in 'is our first universe, a real cosmos in every sense of the word'.[2] We reflected on the reflection of Frank Lloyd Wright that the house, in its 'wooded sward or strand', provides 'a refuge for the expanding spirit of man, the individual'.[3]

Moving inside the house, to consider its internal workings, we followed the famous dictum of Le Corbusier that 'the house is a machine for living in': a well-ordered microcosmos, with a place for everything, and in which everything – every chair, table, bed and stool – has a place.

For such a home – a harmonious composition of architecture, furniture, *objets d'art*, and all the rest of it – forms the house that the architect designed to make our rich man happy. To make such a home is, as Wright wrote, to 'make of a human dwelling-place a complete work of art, in itself expressive and beautiful, intimately related to modern life and fit to live in'.[4]

Such a house should contain only things which aid the workings of its machinery and the composition of its aesthetic order: things that, as William Morris wrote, are beautiful and useful, and are co-ordinated with the house as a whole. Anything else becomes mere clutter, causing, as Danny Miller suggested, 'our relationships to things to come at the expense of our relationships to people'.[5]

And once such a work of art is made, we've seen, it is time to enjoy what has been created, for home, above all places, is a place of rest. Home is the place that, as Bachelard wrote, 'shelters daydreaming . . . protects the dreamer [and] allows one to dream in peace'.[6] That's what all that harmony, all that comfort, all those cushions and curtains are for, isn't it?

And being a place of rest, a little world built, furnished, ornamented and decorated according to our own individual tastes, it may be taken as read that home is a private place. It is the place in which we, like our rich man ensconced in his own little cosmos, surrounded by his family and his things, can be most fully ourselves.

It's a tempting set of assumptions; and repeating them could have made this book easy and comforting both to write and to read. I could have shown you some beautiful houses, some elegant furniture, and some dazzling objects. I could have given you a rule or two for good taste, and given you a labour-saving tip or two. I could have told you to lock the door, put on the mood music, light the scented candles and leave the world behind.

A poor little rich man

But there's another part to the story of the rich man – one I haven't told you about yet. You see, the story doesn't end quite as happily as all that.

Lovely as his new house was, the rich man wasn't used to living artistically; and he did need some training to make himself at home in his new home. For the first few weeks after he moved in, the architect would turn up to supervise him, to ensure he kept things where they belonged in the carefully designed scheme of things.

The rich man didn't mind, or he didn't think he did; but, inadvertently, he found himself spending more and more time out of the house, staying late at work, or meeting his friends in town. When he was at home, looking around his beautiful rooms, he couldn't stop himself shedding a little tear or two for some of the ugly old items of sentimental value the architect had advised him to throw away.

It wasn't easy for the poor little rich man to live in his perfect home, you see; and, I suspect it wouldn't be that easy for us either. You see, the problem with that ideal image of home is that it is just that: an ideal, an image, in a story. As we have discovered in this book, real homes, and the making of them, are quite different.

For a start, only a tiny minority of us will ever be able to build a house for ourselves. Most of us will be occupying an apartment in a building full of others that, as the poet Paul Claudel wrote, 'inside its four walls is a sort of geometrical site, a conventional hole, which we furnish with pictures, objects and wardrobes within a wardrobe'.[7]

And what is more, those pictures, objects and wardrobes won't have been designed for that home but will be like the furniture that Frank Lloyd Wright observed his own clients bringing with them as they 'helplessly dragged the horrors of the old order along after them'.[8] And what is more, once it's there, we'll keep moving it around to get comfortable.

Not that it was ever easy to make home into a work of art anyway, for domestic taste, after all, is not something that can be subjected to the eternal laws of art. Instead, it shifts along with our social relations, with fashion, as fast as we can keep up with it.

And as if that wasn't bad enough, we're all, just like the poor little rich man, the helpless recipients of gifts, the incorrigible collectors of clutter, irrepressible hoarders, whose insatiable appetite for objects makes our homes dissonant, disordered and untidy.

Not that we'd get to enjoy the beauty of our homes even if they were beautiful works of art. Like Mrs Beeton or Joan Rivers, we're too busy doing the dishes and making the beds to wander around them savouring their arrangements.

And even the idea of home as a private refuge is something that has only ever really been available to a privileged few. It is increasingly becoming something of an illusion, as we crowd ourselves into ever larger and denser cities, broadcast more and more of what used to be our private lives online, and spend more and more of our time at work and at play in public.

If this book has taught us anything, I hope it is that home is rarely what we expect or assume it will be. Far from being the 'proof or illusion of stability' that Gaston Bachelard argued it to be, it is the unstable, temporary meeting place of all sorts of things – buildings, furniture, objects, and of course people, all on journeys of their own from one place or time to another.

I didn't tell you what happened to the poor little rich man in the end. It didn't turn out well, but I guess you've guessed that already.

One day, the poor little rich man had a birthday party. His family showered him with gifts, and after the party, he decided to ask the architect around to share his happy day. He welcomed him in, and proudly showed him the gifts he had been given, arranged on the mantelpiece in the salon.

You can imagine what happened: the architect was furious, and berated his charge: 'What do you think you are doing, getting presents given you? Have I not designed everything for you? Have I not thought of everything? You don't need anything else. You are complete.'[9]

And so it was finished. What a poor little rich man, indeed, to be complete, and finished. Perfect.

Thank goodness it's just a story. After all, would any of us really want our homes to be as stable, as complete, as finished as the poor little rich man, and his artwork of a home?

How to make an imperfect home

If this book has one single message, it is that home is not something that will ever be complete. Home is a set of strategies we use to make ourselves at home in a world that, as we have just seen, stubbornly resists the urge to stand still for long enough for us to perfect it.

That building a home does not always involve the construction of a new house does not mean that a house rebuilt or reoccupied cannot possess a beauty all of its own, or, on the other hand, that it cannot reflect the selves of all the people that have ever occupied it. After all, Jung's archetypical alternative to the child's drawing of a house, the one constructed and reconstructed over centuries, would be a wonderful place to inhabit and explore.

And that there isn't a perfect place for everything in the home is in fact an opportunity: for ephemeral, liberating play as anarchic as that of Jacques Tati's uncle, as he subverts a joyless Corbusian machine, reminding us that if homes are machines for living in, it is the living, in all its dynamic, unpredictable complexity, that must take priority over mechanics.

Homes weren't, and aren't, and needn't be works of art. They are settings, as ephemeral as those of the theatre or the fairground, for the little, repeated and temporary performances of our lives, from dining in good taste, a la Elsie de Wolfe, or the carefully constructed *cuisine paysanne* of Bourdieu's petite bourgeoisie. Positive beauty might reside in mathematical abstraction, arbitrary beauty in the eye of the beholder; but décor, like dressing up for dinner, or down for breakfast, is social, as well as personal and conceptual.

Ornaments are not a crime. Like the gifts that his family gave the poor little rich man, the child's drawing brought home for him from the kindergarten, or the old ashtray he could never quite bring himself to throw away, our possessions are not, as they might seem to be at first, the contents of a pharaonic tomb, in which we bury ourselves under our own greed. They are, as we endlessly arrange and rearrange them, what Danny Miller calls 'configurations of human values, feelings, and experience'.[10]

Home is a setting we make and remake, clean and tidy, and make and mend endlessly. It's a sort of work which, if only we could see it, and think about it as such, creates little islands of time, separate from the pressures of career, progress, history, improvement and all the rest of it, which crowd the rest of our lives. Remember that, and you can make, unlikely as it may sound, 'drudgerie divine'.[11]

You'll never really escape the world, not even hiding under your duvet at home. Lock the door behind you, and it'll still be there. You'll still have to go out into it tomorrow morning, or sometime. Privacy doesn't exist in places. Like rest, like the little plays of our lives, like our developing sense of ourselves, like our endless changing needs, and our very sense of where we have come from, it exists in something else.

The author of the 'Poor Little Rich Man', Adolf Loos, revealed the moral of his tale in, of all things, an essay on furniture. He wrote:

> Are we human beings ever finished, complete in our physical and psychological development? Do we ever come to a standstill? And if a human being is in constant movement and development, if old needs disappear and new ones arise, if nature as a whole and everything around us is always changing, should the thing that is closest to a human being, his home, remain unchanged, dead, furnished for all time?[12]

And there are messages we can take away from this tale of home, too.

The first is perhaps the least controversial: it is simply that home is a social as well as an individual idea. This is obvious insofar as home is something we associate with family. It is less obvious, perhaps, that our homes are one of the primary means through which we position ourselves in wider society. This might mean arguing about who has to clean the common stair in the apartment block, or who will cut the hedge along a mutual boundary. It might mean pushing back all the furniture against the wall for a party, or proudly displaying one's most prized possessions in a cabinet, or on a noticeboard on the kitchen wall. It might reside in the ways in which we judge others by their taste in décor, or look anxiously around at the colour choices of people whose culinary judgement we admire. It might mean joining in the washing up after dinner with friends. Home isn't just where we go to escape the world of other people. It is how we live in it.

Secondly, our sense of how we relate to home has shifted fundamentally in recent years: we live in an age in which access is rapidly coming to take precedence over ownership. One could call it a revolution, or a return to ancient understandings of 'the commons' – an increasingly fashionable term. For instance, I find it a great deal cheaper and easier to become a member of a car club than to own a car: I spend less money, I am freed of the responsibilities of care, but I still have convenient access to a vehicle when I need one. In the same way, I'd rather subscribe to Spotify than have a record collection, or rent a TV than own one.

We may live in a world of unprecedented plenty; but in spite of it, or perhaps because we take objects so much for granted, we have become a great deal less interested in the permanent ownership of things than in access to the affordances they supply. It is ironic that in a world where everything is for sale, we end up buying services rather than things.

In an age in which house prices spiral out of proportion to salaries, more and more people are realizing that it may make more sense to rent a home rather than to own one. It's something that has made a commercial sensation out of Airbnb, whose principle is, after all, that we should share our houses round, rather than, like dogs in mangers, sit in them alone. In the same way, a generation who cannot afford to buy their own homes has evolved a culture of rental or squatting, would prefer to buy disposable, repeatable furniture from IKEA rather than polish irreplaceable inherited pieces, and might value the ability to share a JPEG as much as to pass on an heirloom.

And that leads me to the final morals of this tale. They are, I hope, simple.

We are only ever the temporary occupants of the buildings we inhabit, which will almost always last longer than we will.

And our occupations are dynamic, as we shift furniture around to suit our momentary or quotidian needs; and as we endlessly collect, arrange, rearrange, or dispose of all the countless objects that pass through our hands.

Our homes are, after all, nothing more than the ephemeral arrangements, illusory scenery, staged to frame the little plays of our lives.

Or perhaps they are nothing more than moments of respite, in which, in seemingly repetitive rhythms of housework, we step outside the treadmills set for us by the world outside, or seek moments of respite from the glare of public life.

All along, we have worked with the assumption that home resides in spaces, objects, and surfaces. We have assumed that, somehow, home can be found in a place, or that, in making places and things, we can make a home.

And all along, we have found that those places or things that can guarantee privacy, repose, beauty, balance, function and origin are, like the end of the rainbow, just out of reach.

Perhaps that's because home isn't a place, after all. Perhaps, instead, it's a time.

Homework

1. How to Build a Home

What is the very first home you can remember?

Look back and remember. When can you remember it from – how old were you? What did it feel like? Where was it? How big was it? How many rooms did it have? And how were they arranged? Look around the home you have made today. Does it contain anything – any furniture, any objects, or even a sense of atmosphere from that first home? Write down everything you can recall about your first home, and, if you can, try to draw it.

Now return to the present. Does that home still exist? Have you seen it? What is it like now? Who lives there now? What have they done to it? Do you know? Has it influenced the way you make your home now?

2. How to Furnish a Home

Make a camp. Go on: just like you're five years old again.

Think of an occasion to justify it: perhaps you're having a party, or perhaps it's just Sunday evening and you've got a school-night feeling and you're sitting at home. Take the furniture, get a few blankets out, and start off by sitting under the kitchen table. You don't need to do it for very long – long enough to finish a bottle of wine, perhaps – or if you're feeling really keen, spend the night. Take photographs of your camp – and, if you can, of yourself in it, too.

What room did you make your camp in? What pieces of furniture did you use? How did you misuse them: did you turn them upside down, or back to front? And when you were finished, did you put everything back in the same places as before?

3. How to Decorate a Home

I have an interior decorator friend who has a great game. You can play it, too.

She plays it on the picture-sharing website Pinterest (www. pinterest.com), but you could do it anywhere. She's collecting images of her fantasy home. Having spent a life making other people's houses tasteful, she dreams of making one, just one, in really bad taste. She collects photos of hideous houses, awful ornaments, and frightful furniture – it's all going in there. Have a go, do the same for a while, collect all those images together and construct your nightmare home.

And then take a look at them. What sorts of images did you collect? Why do you think that the things in them were ugly or in poor taste? Conversely, why do you think the people who chose these things chose them?

4. How to Collect a Home

Take one room in your house – no more than one, or you'll never finish this task!

First of all, make a list of every object in that room: every chair and table, every knick-knack, every drawing pin. Second, count them up. Third, try to classify them – the categories you use are entirely up to you: indeed, it is important to this task that you make them up yourself. Fourth, once you have classified all these objects, remove them from the list until you just have the categories you divided them into, on their own.

Were you surprised by the variety and number of objects a room can contain? How did you set about classifying them? When you look at the categories you created, which proved useful, and which didn't? Did anything surprise you?

5. How to Keep a Home

I think you can guess what your homework will be for this chapter . . .

I want you to clean the floor. Choose a time when you've got time to do it properly – the time you might normally set aside for watching TV, or reading a book. Make sure you do it as well as you can: if that floor isn't perfectly clean, you're not finished yet. If there are other people in the house with you, invite them to join you. Treat this task as is if it were the most important and enjoyable thing you have to do this week.

How was it for you? When did you do it? How long did it take? Were you satisfied with the result? More importantly, did you enjoy doing it? Did you manage to persuade anyone to join you? Did they enjoy it too?

6. How to Make a Home When You're Not at Home

Go for walk – a walk you usually take.

It could be the walk to work, or the one you take on Saturday morning, to the shops. Take a map with you of where you're going, and where you've been. Mark on it, as you go, the places you might stop at regularly along the way: the place you pick up a coffee, perhaps, or a newspaper. It could be as simple as the place you wait for a bus. Take a photo of each of these places, and when you get home, take a look at them: they are your home when you are away from home.

Why do you choose these places? Why one coffee stand over another? Why one side of the bus stop rather than another? What qualities appeal to you about these places?

Bibliography

Bachelard, Gaston, *The Poetics of Space*, trans. Maria Iolas (London: Penguin, 1964).

Beeton, Isabella, *Mrs Beeton's Household Management: a guide to cookery in all branches: daily duties, menu making, mistress & servant, home doctor, hostess & guest, sick nursing, marketing, the nursery, trussing . . . etc.*, 1861 (Amazon Digital Services, accessed September 2015).

Bourdieu, Pierre, *On Distinction: a Social Critique of the Judgement of Taste*, trans. Richard Nice (London: Routledge, 1984).

Cieraad, Irene (ed.), *At Home: an Anthropology of Domestic Space* (Syracuse: Syracuse University Press, 2006).

Csikszentmihalyi, Mihaly, *Flow and the Foundations of Positive Psychology: the Collected Works* (Berlin: Springer, 2014).

Davies, Michael, *City of Quartz* (London: Verso, 2006).

De Wolfe, Elsie, *Recipes for Successful Dining* (London: Heinemann, 1935).

——, *The House in Good Taste* (New York: The Century Company, 1913).

Eastlake, Charles, *Hints on Household Taste, the Classic Handbook of Victorian Interior Decoration* (New York: Dover, 1984).

Fucikova, Eliska (ed.), *Rudolf II and Prague: the Court and the City* (London: Thames & Hudson, 1997).

Gardiner, Becky, 'A Life in Writing: Selma James', *Guardian*, 8 June 2012.

Herbert, George, 'Teach Me, My God and King', composed 1633, http://www.ccel.org/h/herbert/temple/Elixir.html, accessed September 2015.

Hollis, Edward (guest editor), *Unbecoming, an exploration into the liberating wrongness of interiors* (*IDEA Journal*, 2013).

Le Corbusier, *Towards a New Architecture*, trans. Frederick Etchells (London: Architectural Press, 1943).

Loos, Adolf, selected and introduced by Adolf and Daniel Opel, *Adolf Loos on Architecture*, trans. Michael Mitchell (Riverside: Ariadne Press, 2002).

Marshall, Peter, *The Theatre of the World: Alchemy, Astrology and Magic in Renaissance Prague* (London: Harvill Secker, 2006).

Massey, Anne, *Interior Design of the Twentieth Century* (London: Thames & Hudson, 1990).

Miller, Danny, *The Comfort of Things* (London: Polity Press, 2008).

Orwell, George, *1984* (London: Secker & Warburg, 1949).

__, *Down and Out in Paris and London* (London: Victor Gollancz, 1933).

Perrault, Claude, *An Abridgment of the Architecture of Vitruvius* (1673, translated into English 1691, Paris).

Praz, Mario, *An Illustrated History of Interior Decoration from Pompeii to Art Nouveau*, trans. William Weaver (London: Thames and Hudson, 1964).

Rice, Charles, *The Emergence of the Interior: Architecture, Modernity and Domesticity* (London and New York: Routledge, 2007).

Sparke, Penny, *Elsie de Wolfe* (London: Abrahams, 2005).

__, *The Modern Interior* (London: Reaktion, 2008).

__, Anne Massey, Trevor Keeble and Brenda Martin, *Designing the Modern Interior from the Victorians to Today* (Oxford and New York: Berg, 2009).

Sprouse, Jean, *John Pierpont Morgan, Financier and Collector* (New York: Metropolitan Museum of Art, 2002).

Vitruvius, Marcus V. Pollio, *Ten Books on Architecture*, trans. M. H. Morgan (London: Echo Library, 2008).

Wright, Frank Lloyd, selected by Edgar Kaufman and Ben Raeburn, *Writings and Buildings* (New York: Horizon Press, 1960).

Notes

1. How to Build a Home

1 Vitruvius, *Ten Books on Architecture*, 38.
2 'Taliesin' (1932), in Wright, *Writings and Buildings*, 173–4.
3 Ibid. 172.
4 Ibid. 173–4.
5 Ibid. 180.
6 Bachelard, *The Poetics of Space*, 17.
7 Ibid. 4.
8 Ibid. 14.
9 Ibid. 8.
10 C. G. Jung, *Modern Man in Search of a Soul* (1933), quoted in Bachelard, 18.
11 Bachelard, 27.
12 www.who.int/gho/urban_health/situation_trends/urban_population_growth_text/en/, accessed Sept 2015.
13 Loos, *Adolf Loos on Architecture*, 56–8.
14 Ibid.
15 C. G. Jung, *Mind and the Earth* (1931), quoted in Bachelard, XXXVII.

2. How to Furnish a Home

1 Le Corbusier, *Towards a New Architecture*, 107.
2 Ibid. 110.
3 Ibid. 114.
4 Ibid. 114.
5 Ibid. 123.

6   Ibid. 123.
7   'Prairie Architecture' (1931), in Wright, *Writings and Buildings*, 48–9.
8   Loos, *Adolf Loos on Architecture*, 180.
9   Ibid.

3. How to Decorate a Home

1   Praz, *An Illustrated History of Interior Decoration*, 24.
2   Perrault, *An Abridgment of the Architecture of Vitruvius*, Article 1, ix.
3   Eastlake, *Hints on Household Taste*, 7.
4   Ibid. 8.
5   Ibid.
6   Ibid. 23.
7   Bourdieu, *On Distinction*, 231.
8   Ibid. 68.
9   Ibid. 1.

4. How to Collect a Home

1   Le Corbusier, *Towards a New Architecture*, 123.
2   Sprouse, *John Pierpont Morgan*, 22.
3   Marshall, Peter, *The Theatre of the World*, 74.
4   Ibid. 74.
5   Miller, Danny, *The Comfort of Things*, 1.
6   Ibid. 8.
7   Ibid. 17.
8   Ibid. 18.
9   Ibid. 33.
10 Ibid. 62.
11 Ibid. 1.
12 Ibid. 2.
13 Ibid. 296.
14 Bachelard, *The Poetics of Space*, 4.

5. How to Keep a Home

1   www.brainyquote.com/quotes/authors/j/joan_rivers.html#JhZWckDz
    SvD6ZzTz.99.
2   Sparke, *Elsie de Wolfe*, 14.
3   Beeton, *Mrs Beeton's Household Management*, 8.
4   Ibid. 6.
5   Ibid.
6   Ibid. ref.
7   Christine Frederick, 'The New Housekeeping' in *Ladies Home Journal*
    (1912), quoted in Sparke, *Elsie de Wolfe*, 132–3.
8   Ibid.
9   Selma James, quoted in Becky Gardiner, *Guardian*.
10 Ibid.
11 Paul J. J. Pennartz, 'Home: the Experience of Atmosphere', in Cieraad, *At
    Home*, 54.
12 Beeton, *Mrs Beeton's Household Management*, 7.
13 Pennartz, 'Home: the Experience of Atmosphere', in Cieraad, *At Home*,
    52.
14 Kate Lampitt Adey, *Knitting Identities: Creativity and Community amongst
    Women Hand Knitters in Edinburgh* (unpublished PhD thesis).
15 http://psychology.about.com/od/PositivePsychology/a/flow.htm.
16 Herbert, 'Teach Me, My God and King'.

6. How to Make a Home When You're Not at Home

1   Bachelard, *The Poetics of Space*, 6.
2   Orwell, *1984*, ch.1.
3   Orwell, *Down and Out in Paris and London*, ch. XXXVII.
4   Mark Pimlott, 'Between Everywhere, Connecting Everything, and
    Nowhere', in Hollis, *Unbecoming*, 2013.
5   Davies, *City of Quartz*.
6   Michael Young and Peter Willmott, *Family and Kinship in East London*
    (Oxford, Routledge Revivals, 2011).

7   Moira Munro and Ruth Madigan, 'Negotiating Space in the Family Home', in Cieraad, *At Home*, 60.

Conclusion: How to Make a Home

1   Loos, 'The Story of the Poor Little Rich Man' (1900), in Loos, *Adolf Loos on Architecture*, 49.
2   Bachelard, *The Poetics of Space*, 4.
3   'The Natural House' (1954), in Wright, *Writings and Buildings*, 262.
4   'The Sovereignty of the Individual' (1910), in Wright, *Writings and Buildings*, 106.
5   Miller, *The Comfort of Things*, 1.
6   Bachelard, *The Poetics of Space*, 6.
7   Ibid. 27.
8   'Prairie Architecture' (1931), in Wright, *Writings and Buildings*, 48.
9   Loos, 'The Story of the Poor Little Rich Man' (1900), in Loos, *Adolf Loos on Architecture*, 51.
10 Miller, *The Comfort of Things*, 296.
11 Herbert, 'Teach Me, My God and King'.
12 Loos, 'On Thrift' (1924), in Loos, *Adolf Loos on Architecture*, 180.

Acknowledgements

I would like to thank my brother, who introduced me to The School of Life, and who, along with my partner Paul and my mother, have proved invaluable readers. I would also like to thank Cindy Chan, Zennor Compton, Will Atkins and Laura Carr for their editing skills; Fergus and Zosia Jajdelski for their artistry; and Patrick Walsh, my agent, for all his assistance.

Picture Acknowledgements

The author and publisher would like to thank the following for permission to reproduce the images used in this book:

Page 8 Child's Drawing © Westend61 / Getty Images

Pages 18–19 Another Night of Shanghai © SHX / istock

Pages 28–9 The Game of Hide and Seek by A. Bicci, colour engraving. Italy, 18th century © DeAgostini / Getty Images

Pages 44–5 Airstream Trailer Gathering, United States, 1961 © Underwood Archives / UIG / Bridgeman Images

Pages 48–9 A young girl sits in her bedroom looking at her reflection in a mirror with posters of pop stars including David Essex on the bedroom walls in 1977 © Martin O'Neill / Redferns / Getty

Page 64 Villa Trianon © Manuel Litran / Paris Match / Getty Images

Page 68 Melancholia, 1514 (engraving), Albrecht Dürer (1471–1528) Private Collection / Bridgeman Images

Pages 74–5 Museum Wormianum, Copenhagen 1655 © Interfoto / Bildarchiv Hansmann / Mary Evans

Page 86 Seated bride © H. Armstrong Roberts / ClassicStock / Getty Images

Pages 96–7 Picture Post advert, Vol 61 No 11, p. 42, pub. 1953 © Picture Post / Hulton Archive / Getty Images

Pages 106–7 Vagrants asleep on bench on Thames Embankment, London © Mary Evans / Peter Higginbotham Collection

Pages 118–19 Vision of the Future © GraphicaArtis / Getty Images

Notes

Notes

TOOLS FOR THINKING

A RANGE OF THOUGHTFUL STATIONERY, GAMES
& GIFTS FROM THE SCHOOL OF LIFE

Good thinking requires good tools. To complement our classes, books and therapies, THE SCHOOL OF LIFE now offers a range of stationery, games and gifts that are both highly useful and stimulating for the eye and mind.

THESCHOOLOFLIFE.COM

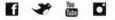

If you enjoyed this book, we'd encourage you to check out
other titles in the series:

Also Available:

If you'd like to explore more good ideas from everyday life,
THE SCHOOL OF LIFE runs a regular programme of classes, workshops,
and special events in London and other cities around the world.

THESCHOOLOFLIFE.COM